International Political Theory

Series Editor
Gary Browning
Oxford Brookes University
Oxford, UK

The Palgrave Political Theory Series provides students and scholars with cutting-edge scholarship that explores the ways in which we theorise the international. Political theory has by tradition implicitly accepted the bounds of the state, and this series of intellectually rigorous and innovative monographs and edited volumes takes the discipline forward, reflecting both the burgeoning of IR as a discipline and the concurrent internationalisation of traditional political theory issues and concepts. Offering a wide-ranging examination of how International Politics is to be interpreted, the titles in the series thus bridge the IR-political theory divide. The aim of the series is to explore international issues in analytic, historical and radical ways that complement and extend common forms of conceiving international relations such as realism, liberalism and constructivism.

More information about this series at
http://www.springer.com/series/14842

Mikael Spång

Emancipation, Democracy and the Modern Critique of Law

Reconsidering Habermas

palgrave
macmillan

Mikael Spång
Department of Global Political Studies
Malmö University
Malmö, Sweden

International Political Theory
ISBN 978-3-319-62889-9 ISBN 978-3-319-62890-5 (eBook)
DOI 10.1007/978-3-319-62890-5

Library of Congress Control Number: 2017947182

Cover illustration: Pattern adapted from an Indian cotton print produced in the 19th century

Printed on acid-free paper

This Palgrave Macmillan imprint is published by Springer Nature
The registered company is Springer International Publishing AG
The registered company address is: Gewerbestrasse 11, 6330 Cham, Switzerland

In memory of my father

Preface

This study addresses Jürgen Habermas' theorising of law, rights, and democracy, as discussed in *The Theory of Communicative Action* and *Between Facts and Norms*. The central issue of the study is Habermas' claim in *Between Facts and Norms*, specifically that his reconstruction of private and public autonomy has an emancipatory aim. This aim makes it relevant to consider Habermas' thinking about law and rights in the light of the modern critique of law, which since Hegel and Marx have directed attention to the limitations of conceiving of rights as vocabulary of emancipation and law as language of autonomy. More specifically, the study addresses the relevance of considering the dialectic of law, law being condition for both emancipation and domination, in relation to Habermas' thinking.

Habermas relies on the motif of the dialectic of law in *The Theory of Communicative Action* in a way he does not in *Between Facts and Norms*. In the former work, he argues that the dilemma of the welfare state law, of both enabling freedom and normalisation, relates in intrinsic ways to this kind of law. In *Between Facts and Norms*, he argues that this is not the case, because the criteria for assessing when welfare state law turns from guaranteeing freedom to normalisation are built into democratic law making, at least when the relation between private and public autonomy is properly reconstructed. Habermas outlines this through a system of rights. This reconstruction is problematic for several reasons, most importantly because it builds on the modern idea of rights, tailored to enable and protect private autonomy. While acknowledging that public autonomy should build on rights of a different type, one that is not tailored to individual choice but to autonomy in the Kantian sense, Habermas faces the problem of showing this other kind of rights. The reason is because there is, at least so far, only one type of rights. All rights, including political rights, are about individual will or choice. It is therefore doubtful whether Habermas can show that criteria for when welfare state law turns from freedom to custodial supervision is inherent to democratic law making. This shows, in my view, the relevance of considering the dialectic of law when trying to understand what rights make possible. In order to be enlightened about the possibilities of rights as vocabulary of emancipation, we also have to direct our attention to the limitations of this language.

I want to acknowledge the important suggestions made by the anonymous reviewer of a previous draft of the manuscript as well as kind assistance provided by Imogen Gordon Clark at Palgrave.

Malmö, Sweden Mikael Spång

Contents

CHAPTER 1

Introduction

Abstract This chapter outlines the focus of this study, taking into consideration Jürgen Habermas' theorising on law, rights, and democracy in the light of the modern critique of law. The latter tradition, going back to Hegel and Marx, addresses the limitations of law as language of autonomy and rights as vocabulary of emancipation. Habermas argues that his account serves an emancipatory aim. For this reason, I argue that it is relevant to discuss Habermas' account in the context of the modern critique of law. This chapter also considers Habermas' theorising of law, rights, and democracy in the context of his thinking more broadly and situates it in relation to sociology of law.

Keywords Habermas · Law · Rights · Emancipation · Democracy Sociology of law

Rights are nowadays central to the political vocabulary and important for emancipatory struggles. For this reason, there is much theorising about what rights make possible. Less considered are usually the limitations of rights with regard to emancipation. However, in the tradition of the modern critique of law, from Hegel and Marx onwards, this question is central. In this study, I draw on this tradition for problematising Jürgen Habermas' conception of law and democracy.

In *Between Facts and Norms*, Habermas (1992) argues that by outlining a system of rights, he formulates the modern promise of

M. Spång, *Emancipation, Democracy and the Modern Critique of Law*, International Political Theory, DOI 10.1007/978-3-319-62890-5_1

self-legislation by citizens in ways that are adequate for functionally differentiated societies. The system of rights is supposed to resolve fundamental issues about the relations between private and public autonomy and the constitutional principles of human rights and popular sovereignty. Moreover, the reconstruction of the basic features of constitutional democracy has an emancipatory aim, reflecting on the conditions of the possibility of 'emancipated forms of life about which the participants *themselves* must first reach an understanding' (Habermas 1992 [1996]: xli).

Stating that we should elaborate on these conditions through the legal medium is not self-evident. To be sure, that law is the language for autonomy is an understanding that several political philosophers and social theorists have advanced. The legal subject and the basic idea of legal equality of persons are central for much of the theorising of freedom and equality in modern societies. The understanding of the political community as a legal community has played a key role in much of modern thinking about politics. Moreover, the understanding of reason as 'legislative', strongly influenced by Kant, is a key idea in modernity. However, we also find much criticism of these ideas in what we can call the modern critique of law. To some extent, this tradition goes back to Hegel. Often, the criticism that rights lead to an atomised conception of the political community stands at the centre of the critique that draws on Hegel. Even though this study relies on certain themes in the Hegelian tradition, more important is the critique that draws on Marx. Often associated with the Marxian tradition is the criticism of law as ideology, but what I find both most interesting and convincing in this tradition is the analysis of the dialectic of law. This entails that law is condition for both emancipation and domination (Buckel 2007, 2009a; Fine 1984; Menke 2013, 2015; Zabel 2015).

Marx acknowledged that legal equality is emancipatory, releasing individuals from status hierarchies and dependencies. Modern law played a key role in emancipation from feudal relations and institutionalising another societal order (Fine 1984). A key element of this order is that legal equality is an attribute of all human beings. Modern legal personhood, in contrast to Roman law, therefore, does not depend on status, whereby was implied the difference between the legal person and the slave: 'Hence in Roman law, even personality itself is only a certain standing or status contrasted with slavery', as noted by Hegel (1821 [1952]: § 40 (39)). Unlike this relative freedom, the freedom expressed by legal personality is the infinite and universal freedom enjoyed by every human being. However, capitalist exploitation is also part of this new order, which for Marx pointed to intrinsic limitations to rights as vocabulary of emancipation. In Marx' case, the reason for suspecting these limitations arose from his observation that capitalist exploitation was compatible with legal equality. Not only are they compatible, but also they seem related to each other. It seems that legal equality plays a crucial role in enabling exploitation because the latter builds on 'free' labour power. Contractual freedom is condition for the possibility of capitalist exploitation (see Buckel 2007, 2009a; Fine 1984; Menke 2013). Thus, Marx criticised the vocabulary of rights, not because he did not 'believe' in rights but because he regarded legal equality and capitalist exploitation as connected in intrinsic ways.

For this reason, Marx thought that modern law is highly ambivalent. He was hesitant to think of emancipation from capitalist exploitation in legal terms. While rights claims were certainly important to labour movements, it was also widely acknowledged that winning rights would not mean the end to exploitation. For instance, Friedrich Engels and Karl Kautsky (1887) argued in their discussion about 'juridical socialism' (*Juristen-Sozialismus*) that the legal perspective is inadequate for formulating the societal transformations that labour movements seek to accomplish. Others followed in their footsteps, notably Otto Kirchheimer (1928), who thought that legal framing of labour relations neutralised and distorted class conflicts (Buckel 2009a; Loick 2014a; Teubner 1993).

Kirchheimer is of interest because Habermas (1981, vol. 2: 524) mentions him as source of inspiration in *The Theory of Communicative Action* when addressing welfare state law as example of the reification he analyses as the colonisation of the lifeworld. Unlike Marx, who focused on private law, Habermas focuses on welfare state law. This is not surprising of course. The welfare state developed out of private law liberalism, dominant at the time of Marx. This involved changes of the relation between private and public law. In the early twentieth century, the democratic constitution was given priority over private law. Public utility, welfare and social and economic equality, articulated in public law, took precedence over private ordering (Habermas 1992: 482ff; Jansen and Michaels 2007; Merryman 1968).[1] Habermas notes that welfare state law is emancipatory in several ways but also normalises in various respects, for instance, forcing individuals to adapt to 'normal' behaviour at work, in family relations, etc. (Habermas 1981, vol. 2: 530ff; Habermas 1992: Sect. 9.2). In *The Theory of Communicative Action*, Habermas (1981 [1987], vol. 2: 364) argues that welfare state law is intrinsically dilemmatic:

> The *dilemmatic structure of this type of juridification* consists in the fact that, while the welfare-state guarantees are intended to serve the goal of social integration, they nevertheless promote the disintegration of life-relations when these are separated, through legalized social intervention, from the consensual mechanisms that coordinate action and are transferred over to media such as power and money.

Habermas' analysis of the dilemmatic structure of juridification in the welfare state builds on his conceptualisation of society in terms of systems and lifeworld, looking at welfare state normalisation as an example of system colonisation of the lifeworld. Habermas (1986) later abandons the colonisation analysis and in *Between Facts and Norms*; he argues that it was too rash to characterise welfare state law as dilemmatic as such (Habermas 1992: 502). Instead, he now understands the problem of guaranteeing and taking away freedom as following from the dialectic of legal and factual equality central to the welfare state. With this dialectic, Habermas has in mind the familiar struggles around the relation between *de jure* and *de facto* equality, in particular, relating to material conditions for equality. Habermas (1992 [1996]: 416) describes this in the following way:

> [M]aterialized law is stamped by an ambivalence of guaranteeing freedom and taking it away, an ambivalence that results from the dialectic of legal and factual equality and hence issues from the structure of this process of juridification. Still, it would be rash to describe this structure itself as *dilemmatic*.

The problem that welfare state law both guarantees and takes away freedom thus remains a problem for Habermas, but the understanding of this problem has changed. He now argues that the proposed reconstruction of private and public autonomy allows for formulating an 'intuitive standard' for judging whether measures and regulations promote or reduce autonomy (Habermas 1992 [1996]: 417).

There are several reasons for Habermas' change, discussed more in-depth in the following chapters of this book. In relation to this change, I focus on two questions.

The Focus of the Study

The first question concerns the dialectic of law, law being condition for both emancipation and domination. This dialectic involves a reversal of how law is condition for emancipation. However, law is simultaneously condition for the possibility of domination. Domination unfolds on the basis of law. Marx' analysis of the relations between legal equality, contractual freedom, and capitalist exploitation is an example. Capitalist exploitation is the opposite of equality, but legal equality is also basis for exploitation. Habermas' analysis of welfare state as dilemmatic is another example. Welfare state law enables emancipation, for instance, through the recognition of social rights. However, these rights are simultaneously condition for the possibility of normalisation. When discussing the dialectic of law, it is central to keep both dimensions in mind. Law is condition for both emancipation and domination.

Habermas' analysis of welfare state law in *The Theory of Communicative Action* takes this dialectic of law into account in ways that he does not in *Between Facts and Norms*. I think this is a problem, in particular, when assuming, as Habermas does, that the legal medium is condition for the possibility of emancipation. In my view, there are reasons for addressing the dialectic of law in the context of Habermas' theorising of law and rights. We need to understand the limitations of the legal medium in order to properly assess its possibilities. This is part of an enlightenment process. Habermas argues in *Between Facts and Norms* that there are no functional equivalents to positive law when addressing how democracy is possible in modern societies. However, Habermas claims much more in favour of the legal medium than its functional suitability. While not thinking that there are normative justifications for law, Habermas (1992 [1996]: 437) makes strong claims about law as language for autonomy, for instance, arguing that legal communication is a 'medium through which the structures of recognition built into communicative action are transferred from the level of simple interactions to the abstract level of organized relationships'. In order to assess both possibilities and limitations, we need, in my view, to take into account the dialectic of law.

The second question concerns whether Habermas makes good his claim to show that private and public autonomy is co-original and mutually supporting each other. Important to the shift from the analysis in *The Theory Communicative Action* to *Between Facts and Norms* is the claim that the reconstruction of private and public autonomy allows us to understand when welfare state law measures turn from promoting to restricting freedom. This claim presupposes, of course, that it is possible to show the co-original relation between private and public autonomy. The modern conception of rights makes this complicated, however. The system of rights Habermas proposes for showing the mutual relation between private and public autonomy builds on the modern conception of rights, tailored as he says to 'freedom of choice' (Habermas 1992 [1996]: 119). At the same time, Habermas recognises that this understanding of rights is not adequate for conceptualising political autonomy. The latter requires 'rights of a different type', rights enabling 'autonomy in the Kantian sense' (Habermas 1992 [1996]: 33—emphasis deleted). It is far from certain that it is possible to bring these dimensions together, that is, rights tailored to freedom of choice, on the one hand, and rights enabling political autonomy, on the other hand. The reason is that there is no other type of rights in modernity. Political rights are like all other rights and not rights of a different type (Luhmann 1981; Menke 2015).

This study builds on the tradition of the modern critique of law, primarily as this relates to the Marxian problematisation of law.[2] Among contemporary theorists, it is important to mention Bob Fine (1984), who in a study on Marx and the social contract tradition developed a very interesting account of Marx and law, Wendy Brown (2000), who has addressed the paradoxes of rights, and Christoph Menke (2013, 2015), who in recent publications on the critique of rights has advanced an account of the dialectic of law that I use extensively. Menke relies on certain features of Michel Foucault's (1976a, b, 1978) analysis of normalisation and Niklas Luhmann's (1981) account of modern law and subjective rights. In addition, Sonja Buckel (2007) has also addressed the modern legal form in critical ways, and Daniel Loick (2014a, b) has taken up dimensions of previous discussions of modern law to renewed examination. The latter includes both early Frankfurt school theorists and the constellation of Marx and Hegel, who are important to this tradition. Also relevant in this context is Axel Honneth (2011) and his discussion of law, freedom, and democratic ethical life.

Structure of the Study

In the following sections of this introduction, I discuss how to place Habermas' considerations about law, democracy, and rights in the context of his thinking more generally. I also address which role to accord law in modern societies, looking at the tradition of sociology of law at the background of natural law thinking, and highlighting similarities and differences between Habermas and Luhmann.

In the second chapter, I attempt to clarify the difference between the dialectic of legal and factual equality as this is outlined by Habermas in *Between Facts and Norms* and how to understand the dialectic of law. The latter focuses, as previously mentioned, on law being condition of both emancipation and domination. In order to situate the focus on this dialectic in the broader context of the modern critique of law, I briefly discuss some major themes in this tradition. In considering the dialectic of law, it is important to keep in mind that this refers to characteristics of modern law. Thus, discussing what characterises modern law and the modern legal form becomes important. I do that in Chap. 2 by way of contrasting Habermas and Menke.

I make use of Menke's analysis of the modern legal form in the third chapter, which is focused on discussing Habermas' consideration of law in *The Theory of Communicative Action*. Since his discussion of law is framed by the analysis of society in terms of lifeworld and system, I discuss these concepts and Habermas' analysis of the colonisation of the lifeworld. The criticism of the colonisation analysis led Habermas to abandon it in discussing normalisation in welfare state law. Since there are good reasons for this, there is a need to account for the dialectic of law in other ways, and I attempt to show how this is possible by way of reconsidering Habermas' discussion of modern law.

I build on this discussion in the fourth chapter, where I address Habermas' reconstruction of private and public autonomy. Discussing the various features of this reconstruction, I point to the problem of bringing together the two dimensions of autonomy. As stated above, the major problem in this regard is that Habermas does not pay enough attention to the fact that political rights are not of a different type than other rights. Because of this, there are reasons to doubt that Habermas shows how private and public autonomy is co-original. In the conclusion, I briefly summarise the main arguments of this study.

Placing the Focus on Law in the Context of Habermas' Thinking

In this section, I address Habermas' conception of law and democracy in his thinking more generally. I draw attention to three themes relevant in this context: the relation between private and public autonomy in constitutional democracy, the understanding of law in relation to the analysis of lifeworld and system, and the importance of subjectivity in modern thought.

Self-Legislation by Citizens and the Promise of Modernity

In *Between Facts and Norms*, Habermas (1992: Chap. 9) argues that the transformation from a liberal paradigm of law, centred in private law, to a welfare state legal paradigm involved changes in the understanding of private autonomy. Habermas (1992 [1996]: 400) argues that what changed was less the normative presupposition, the focus on equal liberty, than the 'perceived social contexts in which each individual's private autonomy was supposed to be equally realized'.

The liberal model was based on the idea of realising equal liberties through the market mechanism and built on the idea of 'the economy as a power-free sphere', as Habermas (1992 [1996]: 400) puts it. Several social movements in the nineteenth and twentieth centuries challenged this model, and their struggles led to the establishment of the welfare state legal paradigm. Materialising rights and establishing new social rights were part of this. As already mentioned, Habermas directs attention to the normalising consequences of welfare state law. In doing so, he, at the same time, advances the idea of continuing the welfare state project 'at a higher level of reflection' (Habermas 1992 [1996]: 410). More specifically, Habermas suggests that this involves considering the internal relation between private and public autonomy. Private autonomy has been central to both the liberal and the welfare state legal paradigms. The result, in Habermas' (1992 [1996]: 408) view, is that both paradigms 'lose sight of the internal relation between private and *political* autonomy, and thus lose sight of the democratic meaning of a community's self-organization'.

This provides the background for Habermas' undertaking in *Between Facts and Norms.* Reconstructing the internal relation between private and public autonomy and showing how they presuppose and mutually interpret each other are central to the argument in this work. Habermas' major point is to outline how self-legislation by citizens is possible. This ambition is, as Matthew Specter (2010) shows, not restricted to Habermas' arguments in *Between Facts and Norms* but has guided him for a long time, from the early writings on political participation, the public sphere, and the early modern revolutions. Habermas (1992: Chaps. 1–3, Habermas 2001) thinks that modern political philosophers have had difficulties to properly elaborate on the relation between private and public autonomy. Some (liberals) have advanced the primacy of private autonomy or the freedom of the moderns, in Benjamin Constant's (1819) words, whereas others (republicans) have advocated public autonomy and citizen involvement. In terms of constitutional principles, we find these ideas reflected in the importance assigned to human rights and popular sovereignty, respectively. Habermas sets himself the task to resolve these tensions conceptually in order to enable the future openness of constitutional democracy.

The fact that we deal with the future openness of constitutional democracy is important. The conceptual reconstruction of private and public autonomy is not foundational. Instead, it is reflexive or captures a reflexivity that Habermas (2001) thinks is central to constitutional democracy (see also Honig 2001, 2009; Thomassen 2008). Specter (2010: 151fff) illustrates this nicely when addressing how Habermas discusses the thorny question of legality and legitimacy in relation to civil disobedience. In the debates about the deployment of middle range nuclear missiles around 1980, Habermas (1983) takes up a middle position between those who argue that civil disobedience is not justified and those who view disobedience as right to resistance. Habermas thinks that referring to the right to resistance is not adequate because that applies to non-democratic states and instead argues that civil disobedience is legitimate when appealing to constitutional norms is what guides the protests against political decisions (see Cohen and Arato 1992: Chap. 11). Specter (2010: 165) notes that civil disobedience shows a '"relationship of tension" between legality and legitimacy that must be maintained if democracy is to retain its open, evolving character'. Keeping this openness of democracy, so that citizens can 'tap the system of rights ever more fully' (Habermas 2001: 776), requires a conceptual clarification of the internal relation between legality and legitimacy. This centres on Habermas' reconstruction of private and public autonomy. The core of the reconstruction is the elaboration of the system of rights.

By the system of rights, Habermas means the rights citizens have to recognise each other when wanting to regulate their life together through positive law. This system of rights includes four basic categories of rights: (1) individual liberties, (2) rights concerning the status as member of a voluntary association of legal consociates, (3) rights regarding the possibility of making claims, and (4) political rights to take part in opinion- and will-formation (Habermas 1992: 154ff). In addition, Habermas (1992: 156f) argues that implied is a fifth category of basic rights concerning the social, technological, and ecological conditions of citizens' equal opportunities to make use of rights. This system of rights is precondition for democratic political processes, at the same time that the more specific content of the basic categories of rights depend on democratic processes of opinion- and will-formation. For this reason, Habermas (1992 [1996]: 122) formulates the categories of basic rights as resulting from the 'politically autonomous elaboration' of them. Thus, rights are not restricting and circumscribing the political legislator in the tradition of natural law. At the same time, rights are not mere instruments of the legislator. In this way, Habermas (1992: Chap. 3) explains, we can understand how, paradoxically, legitimacy emerges out of legality. Political participation by citizens, the ultimate source of legitimacy of law in democracies, cannot work unless legally institutionalised.

Habermas thinks of his undertaking in relation to the transformations since the early modern revolutions, not the least the French Revolution. Writing about the legacy of the latter, Habermas (1988 [1996]: 465) argues that 'there seems to be only one remaining candidate for an affirmative answer to the question concerning the relevance of the French Revolution: the ideas that inspired constitutional democracy'. These ideas are central to the promise of modernity more broadly. Habermas (1985) famously defends modernity and enlightenment as an 'unfinished project', thinking that enlightenment still provides the normative horizon of modern societies and therefore is relevant for orienting thinking and practice. Several of his most discussed engagements, philosophically as well as politically, concern this theme (Habermas 1985; Passerin d'Entrèves and Benhabib 1997). Some critics think that this defence of modernity is both somewhat naïve and less generous to other thinkers than one could expect from someone that stresses coming to an understanding. Regarding the former point, we should, of course, keep in mind that Habermas works in the tradition of the Frankfurt School and is therefore concerned with the dialectic of enlightenment. This dialectic refers to the paradox of enlightenment, producing out of itself its opposite. Max Horkheimer and Theodor Adorno (1944 [1997]: 3) formulated this in aphoristic ways in their first sentence to the *Dialectic of Enlightenment*: 'In the most general sense of progressive thought, the Enlightenment has always aimed at liberating men from fear and establishing their sovereignty. Yet the fully enlightened earth radiates disaster triumphant'. As discussed in the third chapter, Habermas attempts to formulate his own version of this dialectic. This centres on the relationship between the rationalisation of the lifeworld and the development of systems of money (capitalist economy) and administrative power (modern state). These systems could, Habermas (1981) claims, only develop on the basis of the rationalisation of the lifeworld, but systems at the same time have repercussions in the lifeworld, under certain conditions even colonising it.

Law as Hinge Between Lifeworld and System

Habermas is probably most famous for his discussion on communicative action, lifeworld and system. I address this more specifically in chapter three but a few words about these concepts and how law figures in the intertwinement of lifeworld and system are in order before we proceed. By communicative action, Habermas (1981, vol. 1: Sects. 1.3–1.4 and Chap. 3, 1992: Chap. 1) means persons coordinating their interaction through coming to an understanding about something in the world. In doing so, speakers raise claims that what they say is true, truthful or sincere, and normative right. These validity claims are possible to contest and challenge, which either lead to persons giving up on coming to an understanding (resorting to what Habermas calls strategic action of influencing each other in other ways), or to discussions about the validity of what is said. In the latter case, persons enter into what Habermas (1992: Chaps. 1 and 3) calls discourse, addressing claims to validity explicitly and trying to resolve their differences. As will become evident, this idea of discourse plays a key role in Habermas' understanding of democratic lawmaking. Discourses are processes centred largely on debating reasons for and against proposals, suggestions, and so on. Most of the time, the everyday coordination of action through communication geared towards reaching an understanding does not involve dissent but takes place at the background of shared understandings and interpretations. The latter makes up the lifeworld, which is 'the horizon-forming context of an action situation' (Habermas 1981 [1987], vol. 2: 137).

A central feature of Habermas' sociology is that social evolution involves processes of rationalisation of the lifeworld. Norms and values are set free from comprehensive worldviews, such as religion, and become more and more open to interpretation. The legitimacy of norms and values comes to depend on processes of coming to an understanding about them. Habermas (1981, vol. 2: Chap. 6) argues that it is only at the background of this development that systems of money and administrative power develop. System media are generalised media of communication, which transmit highly specific information. Such media allow for connecting action across vast spaces, without those involved in chains of interaction having to work out understandings through communicative action. System media are central for the emergence of a capitalist economy that nowadays encompasses the whole globe as well as for the development of modern states and the international state system. The development of system media enables increasingly complex societal formations. However, system media may also encroach on the lifeworld, even colonising it. This happens when system media replace social integration taking place through communicative action. In *The Theory of Communicative Action*, Habermas (1981, vol. 2: 530ff) analyses welfare state normalisation as such colonisation. Standard interpretations of needs in social programmes and the monetary compensation of risks, which largely redefine lifeworld problems in consumerist ways, are examples.

Law plays a key role in this intertwining of systems and lifeworld. Habermas (1992: Chaps. 1 and 2) argues that law is a 'hinge' between lifeworld and system, both as law channels the influence of the lifeworld on systems and the impact of systems on the lifeworld. In discussing the role of law in the context of the uncoupling of lifeworld and system media, Habermas (1981 [1987], vol. 2: 185) remarks:

> We cannot directly infer from the mere fact that system and social integration have been largely uncoupled to linear dependency in one direction or the other. Both are conceivable: the institutions that anchor steering mechanisms such as power and money in the lifeworld could serve as a channel *either* for the influence of the lifeworld on formally organized domains of

action *or*, conversely, for the influence of the system on communicatively structured contexts of action.

This formulation suggests that we view Habermas' major works in a complementary fashion. In *The Theory of Communicative Action*, Habermas argues that lifeworld rationalisation is a precondition for system differentiation but that systems affect the lifeworld in significant ways. Under certain conditions, the system media of money and administrative power even have colonising effects on the lifeworld. Law plays an important role in this analysis because it anchors system media in the lifeworld and channels the impact of system media on it. In *Between Facts and Norms*, it is instead the possibilities of citizens to influence and program systems by engaging in democratic political processes, such as opinion-formation, legislation, claiming rights, which stand at the centre. Habermas then approaches law as the medium through which it is possible to realise the promise of self-legislation by citizens in modern functionally differentiated societies.

Looking at Habermas' two works in this complementary way gives an understanding of the architectonic of Habermas' reflections about modern law in the context of social theory (compare Deflem 2013; Eder 1988). The understanding of law as hinge between lifeworld and system, which makes law central to the analysis of how system media affects the lifeworld and how citizens may influence the regulation of system media, directs attention to the ambiguity of law. Law is both a medium for the realisation of self-legislation and for the system colonisation of the lifeworld. I think that there are reasons to highlight this complementarity between *The Theory of Communicative Action* and *Between Facts and Norms*, but it should of course also be kept in mind that there are significant differences between the two works. Hugh Baxter (2011) points to several of these in his interesting study on Habermas and law. Most important, Baxter argues that even though Habermas 'officially' relies on the distinction between system and lifeworld in *Between Facts and Norms*, he tacitly abandons it in favour of a communication theoretical conception of society. The latter builds on the idea of the democratic circulation of power, beginning with citizens' political activities, their influencing of legislation in political bodies and the enactment of laws whereby administrative power is programmed and the economic system is regulated. Habermas (1992: Chaps. 7–8) discusses this circulation of power in terms of the generation of communicative power and its relation to administrative power, an understanding that Baxter (2011: Chap. 4) points out, is not compatible with the lifeworld-system analysis.[3]

Modernity and Subjectivity

When discussing Hegel, who was the first to develop a clear concept of modernity according to Habermas, he stresses how Hegel saw 'the modern age as marked universally by a structure of self-relation that he calls subjectivity' (Habermas 1985 [1987]: 16). The Reformation, the Enlightenment, and the French Revolution were central historical events in this regard. The declaration of rights adopted in 1789, the constitutions during the following years and the Napoleonic Code 'validated [for Hegel] the principle of freedom of will against historically pre-existing law as the substantive basis of the state', Habermas (1985 [1987]: 17) argues and continues giving examples from religion, morality, and art of the centrality of the principle of subjectivity. Habermas (1985 [1987]: 18) concludes: 'In modernity, therefore, religious life, state, and society as well as science, morality, and art are transformed into just so many embodiments of the principle of subjectivity'.

Habermas addresses how Hegel's way of noting the centrality of subjectivity in modernity connects to the differentiation of morality, art, and science, which Kant articulated in his critiques of reason and Weber later diagnosed as rationalisation of value spheres, and focuses on the problem Hegel posed. For Hegel, what Kant did not perceive as problematic in his account of reason was 'the need for unification that emerges with the separations evoked by the principle of subjectivity' (Habermas 1985 [1987]: 19). This need emerges when one addresses modernity historically, that is, as 'the dissolution of the exemplary past', on the one hand, and 'the necessity of creating all that is normative out of itself', on the other hand (Habermas 1985 [1987]: 20). Hegel posed questions about the principle of subjectivity that Habermas finds central to the problem of modernity, but ultimately Hegel came to embrace a concept of reason capable of unifying the differentiation of reason that is untenable. This leads us to an impasse, Habermas thinks, because neither is the absolute nor the simple embracing of the principle of subjectivity alternatives. Working out another path, a path not taken by Hegel, even though alluded to, becomes Habermas' task. This path takes us from subject-centred reason to an intersubjective account of it.

Habermas stresses how a different relation-to-self is possible when we begin with participants engaged in reaching an understanding about something and coordinating action on this basis. This relation-to-self is no longer that of an observer to entities in the external world but one in which 'ego stands within an interpersonal relationship that allows him to relate to himself as a participant in an interaction from the perspective of alter' (Habermas 1985 [1987]: 297). This allows for escaping the objectifying relation to self that is characteristic of the philosophy of the subject. Instead of 'reflectively objectified knowledge', we have a 'recapitulating reconstruction of knowledge already employed' (Habermas 1985 [1987]: 297).

Habermas uses the method of reconstruction when accounting for communicative action, building on the know-how that competent speakers already master, and in understanding societal evolution as processes of learning (see Cooke 1994; Pedersen 2009, 2011). With regard to the specific focus of this study, Habermas argues that by reconstructing the system of rights, we can formulate an account of constitutional democracy. The point of the reconstruction is to formulate the conditions of the possibility of this form of government, not by assuming some basic principles but by reflecting on reason established in democratic practices over the past 200 years. Daniel Gaus (2013) points to three elements in this regard, at the background of Habermas' thinking that the rationalisation of the lifeworld leads to increased reflexivity. First, Gaus (2013: 564) stresses how participants, in establishing the framework of constitutional democracy, understand that 'there exists no functional equivalent to the ordering power of the medium of positive law'. Second, the constitutional order builds on modern ideas of freedom, self-determination (autonomy), and self-realisation (authenticity), respectively. Third, participants understand that political processes are fallible, in the sense that what is today regarded as rational may not be seen as such in the future. Central to constitutional democracy are the possibilities of revising laws and regulations, including constitutional law.

The idea that intersubjectivity makes it possible to avoid problems of subject-centred reason guides much of Habermas' theorising. Besides making it possible to escape from an objectifying relation to self, Habermas gives another important example of how an intersubjective account is an alternative, with respect to Hegel's understanding. This concerns Hegel's theorisation of modern society in *The Philosophy of Right*. Habermas (1985 [1987]: 37) notes that since the end of the eighteenth century, the classical conception of politics, encompassing both state and society, has 'split apart into a social theory grounded in political economy on the one hand and a theory of the state inspired by modern natural right on the other'. Hegel stood in the middle of these developments, incorporating political economy in his account of (economic) civil society and adhering to modern natural law when discussing the state. Yet, Hegel remained bound to the classical conception of politics. Therefore, Hegel viewed civil society as moment within ethical life, modelled along the lines of classical politics, and as destruction of it.[4] The result is that Hegel conceived of the state as 'higher-level subjectivity' vis-à-vis 'the subjective freedom of the individual' rather than to view the mediation in terms of 'the higher-level intersubjectivity of an uncoerced formation of will within a communication community' (Habermas 1985 [1987]: 40, emphasis deleted). Habermas believes the latter approach was touched upon in Hegel's early writings, but he did not follow through on this. Instead of a democratic conception of the organisation of society, Hegel opted for monarchy. For Habermas (1985 [1987]: 40), this is not a coincidence, given how Hegel did not abandon the philosophy of the subject: '[T]he logic of a subject conceiving itself makes the institutionalism of a strong state necessary'.

In line with stressing intersubjectivity, Habermas criticises models of politics where the 'self' in self-legislation by citizens is viewed along the lines of a subject writ-large. For this reason, he argues that popular sovereignty does not reside in the people as subject. He contends that 'the "self" of the self-organizing legal community disappears in the subjectless forms of communication that regulate the flow of discursive opinion- and will-formation' (1992 [1996]: 301). While this provides a strong basis for an account of democracy that does not get snared in questions about the people, its constitution and action, there is still the question of how subjective rights fit into this.

The principle of subjectivity is obviously central to modern law, expressed in the notion of subjective rights. As argued by several scholars, the centrality accorded to subjective rights in modern law involves fundamental changes of law (Habermas 1992: Sect. 1.3; Luhmann 1970, 1981; Menke 2015). One important change is the primacy of rights in modern law. This primacy of rights is sometimes understood in terms of the foundation of law, rights being prior to the establishment of the legal-political order. This understanding, often discussed as a natural law view, is usually contrasted with some version of legal positivism. While these controversies to be sure structure much of the modern discussion of law, I agree with Menke (2015: part 1) that the most important dimension to the primacy of rights is how rights refer to what is outside of law. Rights articulate a relation between law and non-law. The outside of law is understood in a twofold sense, as the natural striving of self-preservation, on the one hand, and thoughts and inclinations of individuals, on the other hand. As will be explained, the latter dimension makes understandable the key role that individual will play for modern conceptions of rights. These express an idea of individual will or choice (*Willkür*).[5] This is a concept of will focused on what is individuals' 'own will' (*Eigenwillen*) (see also Luhmann 1981).

What Role Does Law Play in Modern Societies?

An important question to address when wanting to understand Habermas' approach to law and rights is, of course, what role law plays in modern societies. Habermas' reconstruction of private and public autonomy aims to clarify the meaning and implications of self-legislation of citizens in modern functionally differentiated societies.

In general, modern societies being functionally differentiated means that the older models of governing state and society through law, articulated in modern natural law and in social contract doctrines, are problematic starting points. For the social contract thinkers, Habermas (1992 [1996]: 43) observes, law mediated 'all other social relations' and therefore '[l]egal motifs seemed to provide an adequate model for the legitimacy of a well-ordered society'. In similar ways, Blandine Kriegel (1989: 58) notes how the social contract thinkers sought to 'juridify the political sphere'. This application of law went all the way down, so to speak, relating not only to the state but to the fundamentals of the constitution of the political community as such, that is, 'the idea that the law is the obligation of a body politic in its entirety to submit itself and subject itself to juridification' (Kriegel 1989: 62).

Political economy and sociology problematised this type of approach (see Banakar and Travers 2013; Deflem 2008; Habermas 1992: Sect. 2.1; Kelley 1990: Chap. 14; Luhmann 1993: Chap. 1). The early political economists directed attention towards how economic patterns, in Alex Callinicos' (2007: 18) words, 'represented a social objectivity which could not be equated either with political institutions and actions of statesmen or with individual human beings and their self-conscious actions'. Understanding this kind of social objectivity became the task of the political economists and later for the sociologists, something they thought required new concepts and ways of exploring it. The need to consider other mechanisms of integration besides law, in particular markets, did not mean that sociologists neglected law. In the contrary, the study of law has been important in the sociological tradition, partly reflecting the fact that, somewhat paradoxically, accompanying the decline in modern natural law thinking, we also see an emphasis on legislation as mode of governing from the late eighteenth century onwards. As Alan Hunt (2013: 21f) points out, the 'deployment to promote, secure or defend specific social interests, is precisely what was "new" about the legal orders that emerged in the late eighteenth century'. Hunt thinks that the development of this proliferation of laws is important for sociology of law.

Sociologists developed different diagnoses of the changed constellation of law and society in modernity. Famously, Max Weber (1922: Chap. 7) addressed the function of law in modern bureaucratic states, stressing the important role the development of systematic legal knowledge had for rationalisation of law (see also Hunt 2013). In discussing various stages of the development of law, Weber (1922 [1978]: 882) thought that the final stage involved the 'systematic elaboration of law and professionalized administration of justice by persons who have received their legal training in a learned and formally logical manner'. In Weber's view, the formalisation of law served important purposes, notably guaranteeing freedom and making it possible for individuals to foresee the legal consequences of their actions. Thinking that formalisation and rationalisation amount to the same thing made Weber sceptical of attempts to have law serve purposes of social justice and the like. The latter would mean a de-formalisation of law, its materialisation. Materialisation threatens the achievements of formalisation. Closely related to formalisation is also the rise of legal positivism. Weber (1922 [1978]: 874) argued that the combined effects of 'juridical rationalism and modern intellectual scepticism' meant that natural law had 'lost all capacity to provide the fundamental basis of a legal system'. As a result, legal positivism has 'advanced irresistibly', Weber (1922 [1978]: 874f) argued and continued: 'The disappearance of the old natural law conceptions has destroyed all possibility of providing the law with a metaphysical dignity by virtue of its immanent qualities'. The diagnosis of the irresistible advance of legal positivism is certainly an important background to discussions in sociology of law, including that of Habermas and Luhmann, as discussed below. As is further discussed in the third chapter, Weber is important for Habermas' way of addressing the problems of legal positivism and the relevance of modern natural law thinking.

Besides Weber, it is also important to draw attention to Émile Durkheim and the way he discussed law in relation to the functional differentiation of modern societies. Most famous is probably how Durkheim (1893) connected the transition from mechanic to organic integration to transformations of law (Deflem 2008: Chap. 3). However, the details and merits of this account do not need to concern us. Important, though, is the role Durkheim's theorising of law has for Habermas. Two dimensions stand out. First, law is a way of tracing evolutionary changes from traditional to modern societies as well as transformations of modern societies.[6] Second, law is an indicator of social solidarity and allows for understanding how functional differentiation connects to the social integration of modern societies. Habermas (1981) agrees with Durkheim that law must be understood in relation to forms of solidarity in modern society. In one part, this involves taking into account functional differentiation, and in another part, it involves addressing the increase in reflexivity that Habermas (1981, vol. 2: Sect. 5.2) discusses as the rationalisation of the lifeworld. The latter implies that we can rely less and less on an already established normative consensus and instead have to build this consensus on ways of arriving to it. Democratic lawmaking processes fit into this picture because they involve enacting laws on the basis of opinion- and will-formation processes. Solidarity is source of laws but not as given form. Instead, solidarity is outcome of processes of coming to an understanding about issues of societal relevance. However, law does not only enable social integration, it is also tied to systems and therefore to modern societies being functionally differentiated.

Functional differentiation is central to Habermas' account of society, but his analysis is restricted to the system media of money and administrative power. In this regard, he differs not only from Talcott Parsons but also from Luhmann, who theorises modern society consistently in terms of functional differentiation. Besides the economic and political systems, Luhmann also discusses several other systems, such as law, science, religion, medicine, family, sexuality, and so on. This expresses how functional differentiation is key feature of modern societies, replacing hierarchy that was central to previous society. As a result, 'no system of functions, not even the political, can take the place of hierarchy and its summit. We live in a society which cannot represent its unity in itself, as this would contradict the logic of functional differentiation' (Luhmann 1987: 105). Closely related to functional differentiation is the emergence of subjective rights because in pre-modern societies, persons belonged to only one order ('system'), for instance, an estate. Modern functionally differentiated society is different. What 'previously seemed normal is now impossible', Luhmann (cited in Verschragen 2002: 266) notes and continues 'the singular person can no longer belong to one and only one societal subsystem'. Individuals are active in various systems at the same time, in legal, economic and political systems, and so on. Rights enable such participation, regulating access, conditions of participation, etc. (Luhmann 1970, 1981).

Luhmann's perspective makes understandable how most systems are global, although territorial differentiation plays a central role concerning legal and political systems. The consistent theorising of functional differentiation also clarifies that it is not possible to govern society from one system. While most contemporary social and political theorists acknowledge the latter point, much of political theory is still wedded to ideas of the possibility of governing societies through law. Ideas of self-legislation by citizens imply this, at least in some way and to some degree. In contrast, Luhmann's (1993: Chap. 1) understanding of law and politics implies that it is not the autonomy of human beings, legislating their own freedom, which is central to modern society but instead the autonomy of systems.

Looking at Habermas from this perspective suggests that Habermas clings on to conceptions of society that derive from modern natural law and social contract theory. Conversely, Habermas thinks that Luhmann faces the opposite problem. Saying adieu to the model of self-legislation by citizens would mean no longer being able to clarify the meaning of democracy. In a section on sociological disenchantment of law in *Between Facts and Norms*, Habermas (1992: Sect. 2.1) connects the displacement of law by Marx and more generally the influence of political economy on sociology until the development of systems theory. Habermas (1992 [1996]: 48) regards Luhmann as an example of a longer tradition that 'assigns law a marginal position' in understanding society and 'neutralizes the phenomenon of legal validity by describing things objectivistically'.

Discussing the first charge against Luhmann, that is, him assigning law a marginal position, it is doubtful whether this is really the case. Luhmann certainly does not consider law in the ways modern natural law thinkers did. The legal system is autonomous from other systems, such as the political or the economic system. Luhmann (1993: Chap. 2) discusses this autonomy through the concept of autopoiesis, self-production, meaning that systems produce and reproduce themselves through distinctions between them and their environment. Central in this regard is that systems operate through coding of communication. These codes are specific to each system. In the case of the legal system, coding takes place through the distinction between legal and illegal. It is not possible to determine which communications are legal in some external way, but only the legal system can say what is law and what is not law. This self-referential process means that coding matters for both the operation of systems and the distinction between system and its environment (see also King and Thornhill 2003: 35ff).

The way systems are autopoietic may suggest that they are completely closed off from each other, but Luhmann (1993: Chap. 2) insists that they are not. There is operational closure of systems, which is key for them remaining distinct systems, but they are opened to their environments and linked to other systems in several ways. Systems are open in a cognitive sense to their environments, whereby events and processes in the environment become important to the system. Luhmann (1993: Chap. 10) discusses this in terms of irritations and structural couplings. Irritations are more occasional in nature, whereas structural couplings are about making systems responsive to each other on an ongoing basis (Baxter 2011: 184f). As Luhmann (1993 [2004]: 382) puts it, coupling mechanisms are structural couplings 'if a system presupposes certain features of its environment on an ongoing basis and relies on them structurally' (Luhmann 1993 [2004]: 382). Examples of structural couplings between the legal and the economic systems are property and contractual freedom. Legislation and constitutions are examples of structural couplings between the legal and the political systems. Structural couplings both link and separate systems. Constitutions link the legal and political systems to each other but also presuppose their differences and distinctiveness. From the early modern revolutions onwards, the 'constitution has been understood as positive statute law, which constitutes positive law itself and through that regulates how political power can be organized and implemented in a legal form with legally mandated restrictions' (Luhmann 1993 [2004]: 405).

This role of constitutions relates to one important difference between Habermas and Luhmann, namely that Luhmann considers the legal and the political systems as distinct, whereas Habermas does not (Baxter 2011: 84).[7] Luhmann does acknowledge the difficulties of separating the two systems, especially when considering how important the parallel developments of positive law and political democratisation have been for contemporary understandings of law and politics (Luhmann 1993: 416f). The 'unitary view' is understandable from a historical point of view, Luhmann (1993 [2004]: 364) argues, but the more the emblem of this unity, the *Rechtsstaat*, develops, the less plausible the unitary view becomes. The 'concept of the state becomes an artificial device for holding together what has emerged as the self-reinforcing dynamics in the political system and the legal system' Luhmann (1993 [2004]: 365). Politics is not about the ongoing interpretation of the constitution, Luhmann (1993 [2004]: 365) remarks, and the legal system is not only about 'the implementation of political programmes'.

This understanding goes against, if not the details of Habermas' understanding of politics and law, at least the broad perspective that Habermas proposes. Even though politics is certainly not only about interpreting the constitution for Habermas, the constitutional perspective is central for discussing political practices and the functioning of institutions (see also Specter 2010). Moreover, the programing of systems that takes place through legislation follows more or less closely an idea of the implementation of laws through administration and courts. While stressing features both of the legal system, such as the making of law through courts, and of the political system, such as corporatist involvement of interest organisations, which do not fit into the 'constitution-implementation' model, we should note that Luhmann also follows this model in several respects. Law, Luhmann (1993 [2004]: 370) notes, is 'the most important imaginable precondition for the making of politics' because the latter means 'deciding politically which law is to be valid law'. Law performs a vital role for the political system because law makes collectively binding decisions possible. Thus, legislation plays an important role in understanding the structural coupling of the legal and political systems. Legislation is both part of the political system, when considered as decision-making process, and the legal system when we consider, for instance, how legislation involves anticipating the application of laws in courts (King and Thornhill 2003: 44f).

In addition to the question of the relation between law and politics discussed so far, there is another dimension to Habermas' criticism of Luhmann assigning law a marginal role. This has to do with Habermas (1992 [1996]: 56) thinking that Luhmann does not recognise the importance of the legal language for circulating 'normatively substantial messages' in society. While Habermas thinks that functional differentiation makes it necessary to adapt the imaginary of self-legislation by citizens, he stresses that law is a way of communicating problems, issues, etc., throughout society. Law is language for citizens, allowing them to express everyday concerns and discuss them in various fora. When entering parliamentary bodies, 'normatively substantial messages' provide the basis for legislation. Enacting laws, in turn, makes it possible to programme the system media of money and administrative power (Habermas 1992: Chaps. 7–9; see also Baxter 2011: Chap. 4).

Baxter (2011: Chap. 4) thinks that this view of law enabling the circulation of messages implies a fundamental shift with regard to how Habermas used the system-lifeworld distinction in *The Theory of Communicative Action*. Habermas adheres to this distinction, though, when commenting on how the language of law enables the circulation of normative messages. This illustrates what he has in mind with law as 'hinge' between systems and lifeworld. As Habermas (1992 [1996]: 81) expresses it:

> [T]he legal code not only keeps one foot in the medium of ordinary language, through which everyday communication achieves social integration in the lifeworld; it also accepts messages that originate there and puts these into a form that is comprehensible to the special codes of the power-steered administration and the money-steered economy.

Law allows for transforming what citizens articulate in public spheres and through political action into codes that are 'comprehensible' to systems, whereby it is possible to program administrative power and the money-steered economy. For Habermas, ordinary language is (1992 [1996]: 56) a 'universal horizon of understanding' that in principle can 'translate everything *from* all languages'. However, it cannot 'operationalize its messages in a manner that is effective for all types of addresses' (Habermas 1992 [1996]: 56). Law is of help in this regard: 'Without their translation into the complex legal code that is equally open to lifeworld and system, these messages would fall on deaf ears in media-steered spheres of action' (Habermas 1992 [1996]: 56). In line with the understanding of law as hinge between lifeworld and system, Habermas stresses the importance of viewing law simultaneously with regard to system media and lifeworld. Habermas thinks that Luhmann disregards the latter.[8] This Habermas contends means that legal communications lose their 'socially integrative meaning' (Habermas 1992 [1996]: 50—emphasis deleted).

This criticism leads over to Habermas' second objection against Luhmann. In case we do not take into account the socially integrative meaning of legal communication, the conclusion is that legal norms 'lose all connection with the supposition of rationally motivated processes of reaching understanding within an association of legal consociates' (Habermas 1992 [1996]: 50). On this second point, Habermas arguing that Luhmann neutralises legal validity, it is obvious that the two thinkers conceive of legal validity in different ways. For Luhmann (1993: 32), legal validity is not a normative concept but a sociological one. Thus, the question of whether what is valid law also should be valid law does not concern him (see also Thornhill 2011). Laws are valid as long as the legal system recognises them as valid. This is, to some extent, to treat legal validity in an objectivist way, as a social fact. This sociological conception of legal validity connects to how Luhmann (1993: Chap. 3) understands the function of law, law being about stabilising normative expectations. The normative expectation that law stabilises is the assumption that the 'future will *normatively* be no different from the past' (King and Thornhill 2003: 54).

For Habermas, the objectivist understanding of legal validity is an example of sociology becoming too disconnected from modern natural law, an argument Habermas advances not only with regard to Luhmann but also in relation to Weber (discussed in Chap. 3). Habermas thinks that we need both traditions. The sociological analysis is required for normative theories to not be blind to effects of power and the implications of the functional differentiation of modern societies. Conversely, the modern natural law tradition is necessary for the sociological analysis to not be empty in normative terms, as argued by Habermas (1992: Chap. 2; see also Chernilo 2013). This combining of modern natural law thinking and sociological theories is important for understanding Habermas' overall approach. We have to underline, of course, how

Habermas thinks that democracy is central in this regard. It is the tying of modern positive law to democratic processes of lawmaking that is his central point, not tying law directly to moral and ethical considerations of validity of law. This view becomes clear when we address how Habermas, while certainly not endorsing legal positivism, also argues against the 'incomplete' break with the tradition of natural law that has to do with making moral argumentation 'the exemplar for constitution-making discourse' (Habermas 1993 [1994]: 449). For this reason, Habermas (1992: 197ff) discusses how several types of reason, such as pragmatic, ethical, and moral reasons, are important in lawmaking and how compromises reached under conditions of fair bargaining also matter to democratic legislation. As stressed, key to constitutional democracy, Habermas thinks, is that the legitimacy of law stems from democratic processes of opinion- and will-formation.

Underlying this conception of positive law and democratic lawmaking is Habermas' understanding of how lifeworld and law link together. In *Between Facts and Norms*, he introduces law in relation to the rationalisation of the lifeworld. The rationalisation of the lifeworld means that more and more of social integration become dependent on communicative action. This enables reflexive approaches to norms and values. It also enables the reflexivity of institutional complexes, which no longer builds on tradition and custom. However, the more social integration depends on communicative action, the more fragile and unstable it becomes. Habermas argues that communicative action cannot really bear the burden of social integration that falls to it. Habermas introduces law in relation to this problem. Law relieves communicative action of some of its integrative burden and resolves the problem of 'how the validity and acceptance of a social order can be stabilized once communicative actions [has] become autonomous' (Habermas 1992 [1996]: 25). Unlike the spellbinding authority of the sacred in archaic societies, which fused together facticity and validity, the bonding or binding character of modern law is built around the tensions between the facticity and the validity of law. Law does not simply perform stabilising functions but does so in ways that conform to the rationalisation of the lifeworld. Law is an answer to the question: 'What kind of mechanism might allow an unfettered communication to unburden itself of socially integrative achievements without compromising itself?' (Habermas 1992 [1996]: 37).

This study addresses the claims that Habermas makes regarding law, as exemplified in the above statements about lifeworld and law. It does so with respect to the promise of emancipation. This focus is certainly less relevant if we were to follow Luhmann's analysis of law. It may not be completely irrelevant, and there are possibly some affinities in this regard between a systems approach and ideas of 'local' criticism developed from the 1960s, that is, the criticism of institutional complexes and their specific forms of power and domination. While of interest, it is not what I focus on in this study. More important for this study, though, is the way in which Habermas links the Marxian analysis of law and systems theory. While the objectivist interpretation has played a significant role in Marxian analyses, in particular when theorists have relied on the base-superstructure distinction, I do not think that this applies to the analysis of law as condition for emancipation and domination. Addressing the dialectic of law does not entail understanding legal validity in sociological terms only.

Notes

1. Jansen and Michaels (2007: 347ff) argue that European scholars, well into the nineteenth and early twentieth centuries, worked with two interrelated assumptions. First, the idea that 'the validity of all law, including private law, ultimately depends exclusively on the state' (347) and, second, that for 'the substance of rules and principles guiding the relations between private individuals (private law), it was largely irrelevant that the law's validity depended on the state' (347f). On private law, see also Renner (1904). For an impressive discussion of public law, see Loughlin (2010).
2. Habermas (1998: 411f) states that he does not exclude the problematisation of law, but he thinks that doing so requires showing another understanding of law or showing that there is an alternative to law for social integration of modern societies. He says he has no problem with either type of challenge since we 'are not under an *obligation* to regulate our living together by means of positive law', but argues that the discussion of such alternatives has to be 'stated with sufficient precision' to be 'meaningful' (Habermas 1998: 412). This is a curiously strong demand. We may problematise the possibilities of emancipation through the language of law without providing full-fledged alternatives. After all, understanding the limitations of rights as emancipatory tools seems important for understanding what rights make possible.
3. More specifically, Baxter (2011) points out that the interchange model elaborated upon in *The Theory of Communicative Action* is based on understanding the interrelation of lifeworld and system from the point of view of

systems, which is not compatible with the objective of *Between Facts and Norms*, to conceptualise citizens' influence on system media.

4. Ethical life (*Sittlichkeit*) often refers to the particular form of life in a community. The usual contrast is with morality (*Moralität*), which refers to humanity. Habermas (1992: 197ff) uses the terms ethical and moral reasons in this sense. Ethical reasons refer to shared considerations of what is good and worthwhile, shared values and so on, in a political community. Moral reasons, in contrast, refer to all human beings, not what are particular understandings of the good life but what is equally good for every person. Hegel made use of the distinction in this way, thinking that Kantian ethics is concerned with morality. We should, however, note that when talking about community, Hegel stressed the political community. Important in this regard is the Greek *polis*, which for Hegel served as an 'ideal' of ethical life. A central feature of the *polis*, according to Hegel, was that it focused on the close links between ethics and politics, not their separation, and therefore on the role of politics (and law) in ethical education, in the processes of becoming virtuous citizens. This connection to the Greek *polis* is particularly evident in Hegel's early writings. Hegel also used ethical life in his later writings, notably in *Philosophy of Right*, where it refers to the societal relations of family, (economic) civil society, and state. The ideal of the Greek *polis* remains important in this context but stronger emphasis is put on modern institutions central for the actualisation of freedom (see Schnädelbach 2000: 245ff). The latter is important to stress, as ethical life is sometimes given a more narrow culture-oriented interpretation, referring to shared values and traditions. In contrast, theorists like, for instance, Honneth (2011) stress the institutional components. In outlining what he calls a democratic ethical life, the focus is largely on institutionalisation of freedom, including markets and political processes of will-formation.
5. In German, *Willkür* has the connotation of arbitrariness and caprice. Kant (1797 [1991]: 41f) defined this in *Metaphysics of Morals*: 'The capacity for desiring in accordance with concepts, insofar as the ground determining it to action lies within itself and not in its object, is called the capacity *for doing or refraining from doing as one pleases* [nach Belieben]. Insofar as it is joined with one's consciousness of the capacity to bring about its object by one's action it is called the *capacity for choice*' [Willkür]. On the development of the concept of will, see Romano (2004).
6. Habermas (1981) discusses this with regard to law as pacemaker of transformations, both from traditional to modern societies and with regard to the juridification waves of modern societies, from the bourgeois state to the welfare state. I discuss this more in-depth in Chap. 3.

7. As Baxter (2011: 83f) points out, Habermas is unclear on this, but he argues that Habermas 'seems on the whole to favour treating law as part of a more general political system, not as a separate system' (Baxter 2011: 84).
8. For a discussion, see Baxter (2011).

References

Banakar, Reza, and Max Travers (eds.). 2013. *Law and Social Theory*, 2nd ed. Oxford: Hart Publishing.

Baxter, Hugh. 2011. *Habermas: The Discourse Theory of Law and Democracy*. Stanford: Stanford University Press.

Brown, Wendy. 2000. Suffering the Paradoxes of Rights. *Constellations* 7 (2): 230–241.

Buckel, Sonja. 2007. *Subjektivierung und Kohäsion. Zur Rekonstruktion einer materialistischen Theorie des Rechts*. Weilerswist: Velbrück Wissenschaft.

Buckel, Sonja. 2009. Zwischen Schutz und Maskerade – Kritik(en) des Rechts. *RAV Informationsbrief* 102: 11–23.

Callincos, Alex. 2007. *Social Theory. A Historical Introduction*. Cambridge: Polity.

Chernilo, Daniel. 2013. Jürgen Habermas: Modern Social Theory as Postmetaphysical Natural Law. *Journal of Classical Sociology* 13 (2): 254–273.

Cohen, Jean, and Andrew Arato. 1992. *Civil Society and Political Theory*. Cambridge, MA: MIT Press.

Constant, Benjamin. 1819 [1988]. The Liberty of the Ancients Compared with that of the Moderns. In *Political Writings*, trans. and ed. Constant and Biancamaria Fontana, 307–328. Cambridge: Cambridge University Press.

Cooke, Maeve. 1994. *Language and Reason. A Study of Habermas' Pragmatics*. Cambridge, MA: MIT Press.

Deflem, Mathieu. 2008. *Sociology of Law. Visions of a Scholarly Tradition*. Cambridge: Cambridge University Press.

Deflem, Mathieu. 2013. The Legal Theory of Jürgen Habermas: Between the Philosophy and the Sociology of Law. In *Law and Social Theory*, 2nd ed., ed. Reza Banakar and Max Travers, 75–90. Oxford: Hart.

Durkheim, Émile. 1893 [1997]. *The Division of Labor in Society*, trans. W.D. Halls. New York: Free Press.

Eder, Klaus. 1988. Critique of Habermas's Contribution to the Sociology of Law. *Law & Society Review* 22 (5): 931–944.

Engels, Friedrich, and Karl Kautsky. 1887 [1984]. Juristen-Sozialismus. In *Werke*, vol. 21, ed. Marx and Engels, 491–509. Berlin: Dietz Verlag.

Fine, Robert. 1984 [2002]. *Democracy and the Rule of Law. Marx's Critique of the Legal Form*. Caldwell, NJ: The Blackburn Press.

Foucault, Michel. 1976a [2003]. *Society Must Be Defended. Lectures at the Collège de France, 1975–1976*, trans. David Macey. New York: Picador.

Foucault, Michel. 1976b [1980]. *History of Sexuality. Vol. 1: An Introduction*, trans. Robert Hurley. New York: Vintage.

Foucault, Michel. 1978 [2007]. *Security, Territory, Population. Lectures at the Collège de France, 1977–1978*, trans. Graham Burchell. Houndmills: Palgrave.

Gaus, Daniel. 2013. Rational Reconstruction as a Method of Political Theory Between Social Critique and Empirical Political Science. *Constellations* 20 (4): 553–570.

Habermas, Jürgen. 1981. *Theorie des kommunikativen Handelns*, vol. 2. Frankfurt: Suhrkamp. Translated by Thomas McCarthy as *The Theory of Communicative Action*, vol. 1 1984 and vol. 2 1987. Boston: Beacon Press.

Habermas, Jürgen. 1983 [1985]. Ziviler Ungehorsam – Testfall für den demokratischen Rechtsstat. In *Die neue Unübersichtlichkeit*, ed. Jürgen Habermas, 79–99. Frankfurt: Surhkamp.

Habermas, Jürgen. 1985 [1987]. *Der philosophische Diskurs der Moderne*. Frankfurt: Suhrkamp. Translated by Fredrick Lawrence as *The Philosophical Discourse of Modernity*. Cambridge: Polity Press.

Habermas, Jürgen. 1986. Entgegnung. In *Kommunikatives Handeln. Beiträge zu Jürgen Habermas' Theorie des kommunikativen Handelns*, ed. Axel Honneth and Hans Joas, 327–405. Frankfurt: Suhrkamp.

Habermas, Jürgen. 1988 [1996]. Volkssouveränität als Verfahren. In *Faktizität und Geltung, Beiträge zur Diskurstheorie des Rechts und des demokratischen Rechtsstaats*, ed. Jürgen Habermas, 600–631. Frankfurt: Suhrkamp. Translated by William Rehg as Popular Sovereignty as Procedure. In *Between Facts and Norms. Contributions to a Discourse Theory of Law and Democracy*, ed. Jürgen Habermas, 463–490. Cambridge: Polity Press.

Habermas, Jürgen. 1992 [1996]. *Faktizität und Geltung. Beiträge zur Diskurstheorie des Rechts und des demokratischen Rechtsstaats*. Frankfurt: Suhrkamp. Translated by William Rehg as *Between Facts and Norms. Contributions to a Discourse Theory of Law and Democracy*. Cambridge: Polity Press.

Habermas, Jürgen. 1993. Nachwort. In *Faktizität und Geltung, Beiträge zur Diskurstheorie des Rechts und des demokratischen Rechtsstaats*, ed. Jürgen Habermas, 661–680. Frankfurt: Suhrkamp, 1998. Translated by William Regh as Postscript. In *Between Facts and Norms. Contributions to a Discourse Theory of Law and Democracy*, 447–462. Cambridge: Polity Press, 1996.

Habermas, Jürgen. 1998. Reply to Symposium Participants, Benjamin N. Cardozo School of Law. In *Habermas on Law and Democracy: Critical Exchanges*, ed. Michel Rosenfeld and Andrew Arato, 381–452. Berkeley: University of California Press.

Habermas, Jürgen. 2001. Constitutional Democracy: A Paradoxical Union of Contradictory Principles? *Political Theory* 29 (6): 766–781.

Hegel, G.W.F. 1821. *Grundlinien der Philosophie des Rechts*, ed. Eva Moldenhauer and Karl Markus Michel (Werke 7). Frankfurt: Suhrkamp, 1970. Translated by T.M. Knox as *Philosophy of Right*. London: Oxford University Press, 1952.

Honig, Bonnie. 2001. Dead Rights, Live Futures: A Reply to Habermas's "Constitutional Democracy". *Political Theory* 29 (6): 792–805.

Honig, Bonnie. 2009. *Emergency Politics. Paradox, Law, and Democracy*. Princeton: Princeton University Press.

Honneth, Axel. 2011 [2014]. *Das Recht der Freiheit. Grundriss einer demokratischen Sittlichkeit*. Berlin: Suhrkamp. Translated by Joseph Ganahl as *Freedom's Right. The Social Foundations of Democratic Life*. Cambridge: Polity.

Horkheimer, Max, and Theodor W. Adorno. 1944/1947. *Dialektik der Aufklärung*. Frankfurt: Fischer, 2006. Translated by John Cumming as *Dialectic of Enlightenment*. London: Verso, 1997.

Hunt, Alan. 2013. The Problematisation of Law in Classical Social Theory. In *Law and Social Theory*, 2nd ed., ed. Reza Banakar and Max Travers, 17–33. Oxford: Hart Publishing.

Jansen, Nils, and Ralf Michaels. 2007. Private Law and the State: Comparative Perceptions and Historical Observations. *Rabels Zeitschift für ausländisches und internationals Privatrecht/The Rabel Journal of Comparative and International Private Law* 71 (2): 345–397.

Kant, Immanuel. 1797. *Metaphysik der Sitten*, ed. Karl Vorländer. Hamburg: Felix Meiner Verlag, 1966. Translated by Mary Gregor as *The Methaphysics of Morals*. Cambridge: Cambridge University Press, 1991.

Kelley, Donald. 1990. *The Human Measure. Social Thought in the Western Legal Tradition*. Cambridge, MA: Harvard University Press.

King, Michael, and Chris Thornhill. 2003. *Niklas Luhmann's Theory of Politics and Law*. Houndmills: Palgrave.

Kirchheimer, Otto. 1928 [1976]. Zur Staatslehre des Sozialismus und Bolschewismus. In *Von der Weimarer Republik zum Faschismus: Die Auflösung der demokratischen Rechtsordnung*, ed. Kirchheimer and Wolfgang Luthardt, 32–52. Frankfurt: Suhrkamp.

Kriegel, Blandine. 1989 [1995]. *The State and the Rule of Law*, trans. Marc LePain and Jeffrey Cohen. Princeton: Princeton University Press.

Loick, Daniel. 2014a. Juridification and Politics: From the Dilemma of Juridification to the Paradoxes of Rights. *Philosophy and Social Criticism* 40 (8): 757–778.

Loick, Daniel. 2014b. Terribly Upright: The Young Hegel's Critique of Juridicism. *Philosophy and Social Criticism* 40 (10): 933–956.

Loughlin, Martin. 2010. *Foundations of Public Law*. Oxford: Oxford University Press.
Luhmann, Niklas. 1970 [1999]. Zur Funktion der subjektiven Rechte. In *Ausdifferenzierung des Rechts. Beiträge zur Rechtssoziologie und Rechtstheorie*, ed. Niklas Luhmann, 360–373. Frankfurt: Suhrkamp.
Luhmann, Niklas. 1981. Subjektive Rechte: Zum Umbau des Rechtsbewusstseins für die modern Gesellschaft. In *Gesellschaftsstruktur und Semantik. Studien zur Wissenssoziologie der modernen Gesellschaft. Band 2*, ed. Niklas Luhmann, 45–104. Frankfurt: Suhrkamp.
Luhmann, Niklas. 1987. The Representation of Society within Society. *Current Sociology* 35 (2): 101–108.
Luhmann, Niklas. 1993 [2004]. *Das Recht der Gesellschaft*. Frankfurt: Suhrkamp. Translated by Klaus Ziegert as *Law as a Social System*. Oxford: Oxford University Press.
Menke, Christoph. 2013. Die "andre Form" der Herrschaft. Marx' Kritik des Rechts. In *Nach Marx. Philosophie, Kritik, Praxis*, ed. Rahel Jaeggi and Daniel Loick, 273–295. Frankfurt: Suhrkamp.
Menke, Christoph. 2015. *Kritik der Rechte*. Berlin: Suhrkamp.
Merryman, John Henry. 1968. The Public Law-Private Law Distinction in European and American Law. *Journal of Public Law* 17 (3): 3–19.
Passerin d'Entrèves, Maurizio, and Seyla Benhabib (eds.). 1997. *Habermas and the Unfinished Project of Modernity*. Cambridge, MA: MIT Press.
Pedersen, Jørgen. 2009. Habermas' Method: Rational Reconstruction. *Philosophy of the Social Sciences* 38 (4): 457–485.
Pedersen, Jørgen. 2011. *Habermas' Method: Rational Reconstruction*. Bergen: Bergen University.
Renner, Karl. 1904. *Die Rechtsinstitute des Privatrechts und ihre soziale Funktion. Ein Beitrag zur Kritik des bürgerlichen Rechts*. Tübingen: J C B Mohr.
Romano, Claude. 2004 [2014]. Will. In *Dictionary of Untranslatables. A Philosophical Lexicon*, trans. Emily Apter, Jacques Lezra, and Michael Wood and ed. Barbara Cassin, 1234–1237. Princeton: Princeton University Press.
Schnädelbach, Herbert. 2000. *Hegels praktische Philosophie*. Frankfurt: Suhrkamp.
Specter, Matthew. 2010. *Habermas: An Intellectual Biography*. Cambridge: Cambridge University Press.
Teubner, Gunther. 1993. "Man schritt auf allen Gebieten zur Verrechtlichung": rechtsoziologische Theorie im Werk Otto Kirchheimers. In *Der Einfluß deutschsprachiger Emigranten auf die Rechtsentwicklung in den USA und in Deutschland*, ed. Marcus Lutter, Ernst Stiefel, and Michael Hoeflich, 505–520. Tübingen: Mohr & Siebeck.
Thomassen, Lasse. 2008. *Deconstructing Habermas*. Abingdon: Routledge.
Thornhill, Chris. 2011. Political Legitimacy: A Theoretical Approach Between Facts and Norms. *Constellations* 18 (2): 135–169.

Verschragen, Gert. 2002. Human Rights and Modern Society: A Sociological Analysis From the Perspective of Systems Theory. *Journal of Law and Society* 29 (2): 258–281.

Weber, Max. 1922. *Wirtschaft und Gesellschaft. Grundriss der verstehenden Soziologie*, ed. Johannes Winckelmann. Tübingen: J C B Mohr, 1972. Translated by Ephraim Fischoff et al. as *Economy and Society. An Outline of Interpretive Sociology*, ed. Guenther Roth and Claus Wittich. Berkeley: University of California Press, 1978.

Zabel, Benno. 2015. Autonomie und Autorität. Über Emanzipations- und Entfremdungsprozesse des Rechts. *Archiv für Rechts- und Sozialphilosophie* 101 (4): 525–537.

CHAPTER 2

The Dialectic of Law and the Modern Legal Form

Abstract This chapter discusses the dialectic of law and the modern legal form. The dialectic of law, important in the tradition of the modern critique of law, entails that law is both a condition for emancipation and domination. Habermas' analysis of the dilemmatic structure of welfare state law in *The Theory of Communicative Action* addresses this dialectic in ways that he does not in *Between Facts and Norms*. In the latter work, Habermas instead discusses the dilemma of welfare state law at the background of the dialectic of legal and factual equality. I discuss the difference between this understanding and the dialectic of law.

Keywords Habermas · Menke · Dialectic · Law · Legal form

Introduction

By stressing the inherently dilemmatic structure of welfare state law in *The Theory of Communicative Action*, Habermas advances the interpretation that this law both enables and takes away freedom. In *Between Facts and Norms*, he argues it was too rash to characterise welfare state law as dilemmatic as such. Habermas instead thinks that the normalising consequences of welfare state law are understandable in the background of what he calls the dialectic between legal and factual equality.

In this chapter, I clarify the difference between the dialectic between legal and factual equality and the dialectic of law. The major difference

M. Spång, *Emancipation, Democracy and the Modern Critique of Law*, International Political Theory, DOI 10.1007/978-3-319-62890-5_2

between these two accounts concerns whether limitations regarding emancipation are intrinsic to law or not. The dialectic of law analysis implies that it is. Habermas' analysis of welfare state law as dilemmatic is an example of this kind of analysis. The analysis of the dialectic of legal and factual equality is different, not because it does not address normalisation but because the criteria for assessing when measures turn from promoting equality and freedom to its opposite are internal to democratic law, when properly reconstructed. Habermas argues that the reconstruction of private and public autonomy gives us standards for assessing when measures are promoting autonomy and when restricting it. For this reason, the analysis of the dialectic of legal and factual equality does not imply that limitations regarding emancipation are intrinsic to the law in the way that the dialectic of law does.

As suggested in the introduction, I think that Menke's analysis is helpful in understanding the dialectic of modern law. His account builds on analysing the modern form of rights and the modern legal form. I therefore discuss how to understand the modern legal form, contrasting the accounts of Habermas and Menke. Both authors stress the primacy of rights in modern law and note how this initially developed in relation to private law. Yet, they also differ in several respects, among others in how Menke puts emphasis on rights relating to what is outside of law, non-law. This gives the modern understanding of subjective rights its specific characteristics. Menke suggests that the relation between law and non-law is one of self-reflection, thus, relying on certain elements of Luhmann's characterisation of modern law.

The Dialectic of Legal and Factual Equality

In *Between Facts and Norms*, Habermas (1992: Chap. 9.2) advances the argument that the ambivalence of welfare state law relates to the dialectic between legal and factual equality. This dialectic refers to the adoption of measures and regulations that aim towards achieving de facto equal opportunities, central for the development of welfare state law in the twentieth century. However, this development is also ambivalent, Habermas (1992 [1996]: 416) argues:

> [S]atisfying the material preconditions for an equal opportunity to exercise individual liberties alters living situations and power positions in such a way that the compensation for disadvantages is associated with forms of

> tutelage that convert the intended *authorization* for the use of freedom into a *custodial supervision*.

Habermas (1992 [1996]: 416) gives some examples of when this happens, for instance, 'when statutory regulations on work and family life *force* employees or family members to conform their behaviour to a "normal" work relation or a standard pattern of socialization' or when recipients pay for compensations 'with dependence on normalizing intrusions by employment offices, welfare agencies, and housing authorities'. Habermas (1992 [1996]: 416) also highlights problems of collective bargaining when the representation of interests is bought at the expense of 'freedom to decide by organisation members'. These examples are similar to those Habermas gives in *The Theory of Communicative Action* about the colonisation of the lifeworld, but he no longer thinks that they point to an inherent dilemma of welfare state law. In *Between Facts and Norms*, Habermas concludes that it would be too rash to conclude that the dilemma he points to is inherent in welfare state law.

The reason for this change partly relates to Habermas abandoning the colonisation analysis and partly to the fact that he thinks that the 'criteria by which one can identify the point where empowerment is converted into supervision are, even if context-dependent and contested, not arbitrary' (Habermas 1992 [1996]: 416). More specifically, this refers to the reciprocal relation between private and public autonomy, which gives 'an intuitive standard' for judging whether measures and regulations promote or reduce autonomy (Habermas 1992 [1996]: 417). There are two dimensions to this, one having to do with political autonomy and the other referring to private autonomy.

Discussing this in terms of the reconstruction of private and public autonomy suggests that we should look at political processes of legislation and policy making for understanding when measures turn from promoting autonomy to its opposite. Normalisation would then arise as consequence of citizens not being involved in outlining measures, their focus and contents, their implementation, and so on.[1] In this case, normalisation is understandable in the background of political autonomy, more specifically citizens lacking appropriate ways to take part in political processes. Besides this interpretation, Habermas also discusses normalisation with regard to private autonomy. He argues that normalisation takes place 'when welfare regulations, employing criteria of equal treatment in an attempt to secure an actual equality in living situations and power positions, achieve this goal only under conditions or with instruments that... also severely *limit* the vulnerable areas in which individuals can autonomously pursue a private life plan' (Habermas 1992 [1996]: 416). This argument differs from the first one. The fact that Habermas makes this interpretation as well is of course not surprising, in particular, given the importance of private autonomy for the modern conception of rights. However, it partly runs counter to Habermas' argument that the reconstruction of the relation between private and public autonomy creates standards for assessing normalisation.

Stating that the criteria for assessing the adverse consequences of normalisation build on the reconstruction of private and public autonomy is in line with the overall argument in *Between Facts and Norms.* Habermas (1992: Chaps. 7–9) stresses the need for public debates about what are relevant societal circumstances to address when working out laws and policies aiming to achieve equal freedom.[2] Following the proceduralist approach, Habermas (1992: Chap. 9) advances that one has to judge on a case-to-case basis whether achieving equal opportunities requires one to treat cases similarly or differently. Feminist discussions of the equality/difference dilemma show this. For Habermas, discussions about whether to stress equal or different treatment depend on assessing 'which differences between the experiences and living situations of (specific groups of) women and men become relevant for an equal opportunity to take advantage of individual liberties' (Habermas 1992 [1996]: 425). The proceduralist approach opens up for interpreting equality and difference in new ways (see also Johnson 2001). Yet, there are reasons to inquire into the background conditions for this appearing as a problem with respect to feminist politics of equality in the first place.

To some extent, this has implications for the medium at hand, namely law and rights. An example is how Wendy Brown (2000: 232) elaborates on paradoxes of rights, arguing that a key paradox 'is that rights that entail some specification of our suffering, injury, or inequality lock us into the identity defined by our subordination, while rights that eschew this specificity not only sustain the invisibility of our subordination, but potentially even enhance it' (see also Brown 1995). Brown connects this to other themes familiar in the modern critique of law, for instance, that rights mitigate consequences of subordination but does not eliminate domination. She also draws attention to the problem of addressing intersectionality in law, that is, the difficulty of addressing 'subjects marked by more than one form of social power (race, gender, age, sexual orientation, disability) at a time' (Brown 2000: 235). The latter has a specific bearing on Habermas' suggestion to deal with equality and difference on a case-by-case basis. In a specific case, it is likely that there are several differences that are relevant to consider. This, at least, complicates how to assess whether treating cases similarly or differently best advances substantial equality.

The Dialectic of Law

A way to understand how the modern critique of law relates to the point Habermas makes about the dialectic of legal and factual equality is to draw attention to Weber's (1922: 439f) discussion about freedom and coercion regarding relations between workers and capitalists.

Weber noted that the expansion of contractual relations in modern society depends on developments of modern law. However, the extent to which this also means 'an actual increase of the individual's freedom to shape the conditions of his own life' is less certain, Weber (1922 [1978]: 729) thought. In order to assess the latter, we have to look at whether these possibilities are available to all. 'Such availability', Weber (1922 [1978]: 729) continued, 'is prevented above all by the differences in the distribution of property as guaranteed by law':

> The formal right of a worker to enter into any contract whatsoever with any employer whatsoever does not in practice represent for the employment seeker even the slightest freedom in the determination of his own conditions of work, and it does not guarantee him any influence on this process. (Weber 1922 [1978]: 729)

We may interpret this problem along the familiar lines of the distinction between *de jure* and *de facto* opportunities, that is, in the light of what Habermas discusses as the dialectic between legal and factual equality. However, it is also possible to interpret it in ways that are closer to the tradition of the modern critique of law (see Menke 2015: 277ff). When Weber addressed this question, he did so by talking about freedom and coercion (*Zwang*). More specifically, he argued that the question is how to interpret contractual freedom in relation to coercion in one legal community compared to another, 'for instance, one organized along "socialist" lines' (Weber 1922 [1978]: 730). It is true that formally, the 'increasing significance of freedom of contract' represents a 'decrease of coercion' (Weber 1922 [1978]: 730). However, taking into account actual opportunities of making use of these possibilities implies for Weber (1922 [1978]: 730) that 'the exact extent to which the total amount of "freedom" within a given legal community is actually increased depends entirely upon the concrete economic order and especially on the property distribution'.

Discussing this in terms of freedom and coercion suggests not only linking legal and economic orders but also taking into account both dimensions when assessing whether contractual freedom overall implies a decrease in coercion in the legal community. Thus, Weber (1922 [1978]: 730) thought that coercion in a capitalist economy has a peculiar form: 'In this type of coercion the statement "*coactus voluit*" applies with peculiar force just because of the careful avoidance of the use of authoritarian forms' (Weber 1922 [1978]: 730).[3]

Weber's argument about coactus voluit entails considering law in ways that allow us to understand how legal regulations may simultaneously enable freedom and be a condition for domination. Marx viewed private law in this way. As Bob Fine (1984: 119) pointed out in his discussion of how Marx abandoned the analogy between slavery and the conditions of workers in capitalism, Marx came to recognise that capitalist exploitation is 'compatible with—not at odds with—juridic freedom and equality'. In private law, this equality centres on private property and contractual freedom. Market exchange was the medium for their realisation. The early modern social contract thinkers thought that '[n]atural rights will find their reliable counterpart in the laws of trade and commerce' (Habermas 1963 [1973]: 95). Marx confronted this constellation in his problematisation of law. When arguing that exchange relations are 'a very Eden of the innate rights of man', Marx (1867 [1992]: 280) only took the social contract thinkers at their words.

Specific to capitalist relations are that they build on the selling and buying of labour power. This presupposes the legal equality of the bearer of this labour power. Legal equality is therefore the condition for exploitation. The bourgeois private law is a legal order that expresses both legal equality of persons and mechanisms that enable social domination (Menke 2015: 272ff). It has been common to understand this as ideology, legal equality only covering up what are unequal power relations. While there certainly is an ideological element, helping to sustain a certain presumption of equality in spite of its reversals, legal equality is not only (not primarily) ideology, rather it is a condition for the possibility of domination. Capitalist exploitation can develop only on the basis of legal equality. Without legal equality, selling of labour power is impossible. Only based on the active use of rights in private law can persons be exploited (Menke 2015: 289).

Thus, legal equality plays a key role in enabling capitalist exploitation. To some extent, of course, exploitation is the reversal of equality. It is the opposite of equality and a mechanism for generating inequalities over time, but the important point with regard to private law is that this reversal takes place within law. The central legal means of private law, in particular, contractual freedom, is key for understanding how the reversal happens without violating private law. This does not mean that legal equality is not also emancipatory. To be sure, it has been difficult in much of Marxian theorising about law to keep both of these things in mind (see Collins 1982; Fine 1984; Kelley 1978). The problem is that it is neither possible to disregard the legal institutionalisation of equal freedom, to debunk it as mere semblance, nor is it possible to envision the struggle for emancipation only in legal terms, as that which is not yet achieved. The result, Fine (1984: 120) noted, is a deep ambivalence about the potential for liberation through rights:

> Marx never overcame his ambivalence between his conception of bourgeois equality and freedom as "only a semblance and a deceptive semblance" and his realization that "this semblance exists nevertheless as an illusion on his [the worker's] part and to a certain degree on the other side, and thus essentially modifies his relation by comparison to that of workers in other modes of production".

Addressing this kind of ambivalence is central in much of critical thinking about rights and law, from Marx until our own times (see Brown 2000; Buckel 2007, 2009a, b; Loick 2014a, b; Menke 2015; Parla 2011).

Of course, we may think that this ambivalence is due to the inability to come to terms with modern law. In that case, the ambivalence appears as a fault in properly understanding law as a language for the realisation of autonomy (compare Baynes 2000). In part, this is what Habermas implies in shifting from considering welfare state law as dilemmatic in itself to arguing that the criteria for normalisation are found in democratic lawmaking. Habermas also advances a similar type of claim in other respects as well. It is, for instance, implied in his criticism of Foucault's analysis of normalisation, Habermas (1992 [1996]: 79) arguing that 'a sociology that would remain sensitive to tensions of this sort must not renounce a rational reconstruction of civil rights from the internal perspective of the legal system'. Besides Habermas misunderstanding the objectives of Foucault's analysis, I am not convinced that Habermas is able to show that understanding normalisation presupposes the reconstruction he proposes.[4] Moreover, Habermas is less than clear about this reconstruction and its use for assessing normalisation, as already pointed out. While arguing that the reconstruction gives us intuitive standards for assessing when welfare state measures turn from promoting to restricting freedom, he also relies on private autonomy as an independent criterion. The latter is not surprising but the more troubling with regard to the argument that it is the reconstruction between private and public autonomy that gives us the criteria for assessing problems of welfare state law. This points to the problem of building the reconstruction of political autonomy on rights in the modern sense. I have already pointed to some dimensions of this problem and will discuss it in the next chapters.

In general, much of Habermas' arguments about standards of criticism are understandable in the background of an argument he put forward in early discussions about ideology critique. Habermas (1962: Parts 3 and 4) argued that such criticism should not be understood as invalidating the ideas and norms addressed. Instead, one should understand this criticism building on these ideas and how they are used to point to inequalities and injustices in society. Otherwise, criticism would lack direction, and it would not be clear about its own premises. Habermas' argument was, of course, a valuable corrective to certain strands of Marxist ideology critique. Looking at the focus of this study, the implication of Habermas' argument is that critique of domination (as exemplified above with respect to Foucault) requires taking legal equality and rights as presuppositions for criticism to have direction and clarity.[5]

However, addressing domination in terms of the dialectic of law does not invalidate that rights also serve emancipatory purposes. It does, however, imply that we also need to address how domination unfolds on the basis of rights, not only or always in contradiction to them. Rights being condition both for emancipation and for domination is what makes modern law ambivalent. Thus, the dialectic of law suggests that we consider another possibility than separating what explains domination and what enables emancipation. It suggests that we address how domination is the reversal of legal equality and freedom and yet, simultaneously, unfolding on the basis of law. The problem of not being able to resolve the tension between law as semblance of liberation and vehicle for achieving emancipation is then less a fault attributable to inconsistencies and tensions of thinking. Instead, this ambivalence expresses contradictions of the modern legal form, the way in which the legal form both enables emancipation and is the basis for social domination (Buckel 2007, 2009a; Fine 1984; Menke 2015).

Marx primarily addressed the ambiguity of the private law, the institutionalisation of property rights and individual freedom of contract, and so on, arguing that while this allows for one to contest rights (right against right), it does not enable the more fundamental transformation he envisioned in the socialist revolution. There are reasons to stress the importance of private law, both for the development of modern law and for the modern idea of rights. Without taking this into account, the Marxian criticism of law becomes impossible to understand. Marx is certainly not critical of rights because he does not 'believe' in them, because he is sceptical of rights as such. Rather, it is their ambiguous role, how they are compatible with capitalist exploitation and in fact make up an element of the condition for the possibility of exploitation that is at the centre of his attention. Yet, Marx' focus on the private law made him misunderstand the struggles about which kind of law, private law or social law, should prevail. Marx overlooked the development of social law, Menke (2013, 2015: 281ff) argues, which had consequences for Marx' understanding of what the struggles for shorter working days, better working conditions and social protection, and so on entailed. Marx did not understand that these struggles involved claims of a right to life and the recognition of partaking in social life and instead interpreted them as private law claims.

The neglect of social law also had consequences for the understanding of social domination. In social law or welfare state law, domination takes the shape of normalisation, not exploitation (Menke 2015: 285ff). There are thus reasons to attend to how the dialectic of law in welfare state law is different from its shape in private law. Habermas understands this very well. In fact, the reason for him focusing on welfare state law as an example of colonisation of the lifeworld was largely that this allowed him to show the relevance of critical theory in the context where orthodox Marxism was not well equipped to make sense of the welfare state. Even though the specific way in which Habermas developed this turns out to be problematic, the guiding thread of the analysis that we deal with processes of normalisation and these tie in with characteristics of welfare state law seems to me to be on the spot. When Habermas analyses normalisation in *The Theory of Communicative Action,* he does so in ways that point to the dialectic of law, showing how welfare state law simultaneously enables and restricts freedom. I will come back to this analysis in the next chapter, discussing how it is possible to develop it in terms of Menke's analysis of the modern legal form instead of Habermas' analysis of lifeworld colonisation by systems.

The Modern Critique of Law

The dialectic of law is not the only way through which the ambiguities of modern law have been discussed. In order to situate the account of the dialectic of law, I briefly discuss some other central themes of the modern critique of law in this section (see Brown and Halley 2002; Buckel 2009a; Hutchinson and Monahan 1984; Kelley 1978; Kennedy 1985, 2002; Peters 1991: Part 5; Unger 1986). Doing so, I stress the Marxian background to the modern critique of law, paying less attention to its Hegelian dimensions (compare Fine 2001).

An important issue in much of legal analysis concerns the indeterminacy of law, that is, the problem, in Habermas' (1992 [1996]: 199) words, of how to guarantee '*the certainty of law* and its *rightness*'. While important for questions about the legitimacy of law, the debate on indeterminacy focuses primarily on the application of the law. There is an extensive discussion about these issues, but I will leave it aside in the following (see Frankenberg 2009: 106ff; Kress 1989; Unger 1986). Scholars in the tradition of critical legal studies sometimes connect indeterminacy to the analysis of the political conjuncture. Mark Tushnet (1989), for instance, addresses how appeals to rights and their expansion depend on the political forces that enable the recognition of rights and sustain their applicability. Social movements and civil society organisations are important for the recognition of rights, not only initially but also over time. Unless supported by political forces, Tushnet (1989: 409) noted that 'there is little reason to believe that, inertia aside, the right will continue to be recognized'. This is an important point and unfortunately, it often plays a subordinate role in much of legal–political analysis. However, it is not what I focus upon in this study.

Another central theme in the tradition of the modern critique of law is that law glosses over inequalities and power relations. This glossing over makes law ideological (see Buckel 2009b; Fine 2013; Hunt 1985).

To some extent, this effect of rights stems from them abstracting from the societal conditions in which rights function (Buckel 2007, 2009a). Anatole Frances' famous quip about sleeping under the bridges of Paris captures this problem. Related to this is another dimension of the ideological dimension of law and rights, specifically, that they express particular societal perspectives and ideals, such as bourgeois ideas or masculinist conceptions (see Collier 1995; Fine 2013; MacKinnon 1989).

Connected to the charge that law is ideological, creating the semblance of equality, sometimes but not always, attempts to analyse the emergence of modern law. Examples include several types of Marxian accounts of law, which tie law to the emergence of capitalism (Buckel 2009b; Collins 1982; Fine 1984, 2013; Poulantzas 1978: 86ff). One of the most important theorists in this tradition is Evgeny Pashukanis (1924 [1989]: 113), who analysed the interrelationship between private law and relations of production: 'The social relation which is rooted in production presents itself simultaneously in two absurd forms: as the value of commodities, and as man's capacity to be the subject of rights'. Pashukanis discussed the emergence of the legal subject in relation to the shift from the feudal to the capitalist economy, stressing the homologies between legal equality and exchange but also pointing out the specific roles of contracts and the settlement of disputes in this regard (see also Balbus 1977). Pashukanis did not view the law as an epiphenomenon and instead stressed that law is a specific social form. However, he did not fully overcome the Marxist base-superstructure argument. For Pashukanis, the legal form emerged in relation to capitalist exchange, and his account of the subject of right exclusively ties it to private law. Later, theorists who wanted to develop a materialist account of law often drew on Pashukanis, in particular, the idea of law as form, while attempting to overcome the problems involved in the reduction in the form to exchange and the privileging of private law.

Buckel's (2007) analysis of the modern legal form as technology of subjectivation and cohesion is an example. Buckel (2007: 237) stresses that the legal form is a social form in its own right, related to but not reducible to other social forms. Similar to Habermas, Buckel understands the mode of subjectivation in the modern legal form, in terms of the abstraction from concrete life contexts. This abstraction enables the 'commensuration' of interests and understandings of the good life between legal subjects, more specifically the kind of commensuration that allows for interests and ideas about what is good and worthwhile to coexist. This also means that legal subjects relate to each other in an external fashion. In this sense, Buckel (2007: 237f) argues, law is also a technology of cohesion. As technology of cohesion, modern law establishes a mode of formal cohesion between abstract individuals. Buckel (2007) argues that in order to understand the effects of this modern legal form, how law is mode of subjectivation and technology of cohesion, we have to pay attention to how persons use legal reasoning and make legal claims. We need to investigate how individuals seek the redress of injustices, claiming equality or freedom, seeking the resolution of conflicts, establishing contracts, and so on, through the legal language. Buckel is, in particular, interested in how persons make use of this legal language in the context of courts and other legal bodies, where lawyers, judges, and other legal experts play a central role. Even though not drawing on Pierre Bourdieu's (1987) analysis of the juridical field, Buckel's (2007: 240ff) analysis has several similarities with the way that Bourdieu stressed that this field is one of practices, jurists making use of legal knowledge in addressing grievances, building cases, engaging in legal argumentation, and the like. It is through legal procedures and legal argumentation that law has real effects. Even though this allows for expressing and formulating grievances, making claims, and so on, the legal language also has specific formative effects. Similar to how Nicos Poulantzas (1978: 89f) thought that ordinary people have little command of judicial knowledge, Buckel (2007: 240ff) also stresses that it is largely through legal procedures that actors lose 'control' over how their concerns are addressed. Practically, this takes place through the need to formulate concerns in legal categories and to understand themselves in such terms. Thereby, an understanding of persons and their relations to each other that define human beings as legal beings is constituted. It is in this regard that it makes sense to talk about 'legal fetishism', as argued by Buckel (2007: 242f). Yet, fetishism is not illusion. Central to fetishism, Marx (1867 [1992]: 165) asserts, is that relations 'appear as they are'. The latter involves the common understanding that legal relations are actually specific and concrete. Thus, the fetish character of law entails that it takes on ontological meaning, defining human beings as legal beings (Marx 1843b: 231f).

Buckel (2007) argues that we should focus on understanding the structuring effects of the modern legal form. Several other scholars stress the importance of analysing the formative force of law. One common focus in this regard is the formative force of law as it relates to modern conceptions of the subject. An example is how Judith Butler (1990: 2) argues that 'law produces and then conceals the notion of "a subject before the law" in order to invoke that discursive formation as a naturalised foundational premise that subsequently legitimates that law's own regulatory hegemony'. Even though not every theorist would agree with this specific understanding, the force and violence involved in becoming a legal subject is something several theorists point to (Buckel 2009a). More generally, the connection between violence and law has attracted wide attention, famously in the way that Walter Benjamin (1921) analysed the intertwining of lawmaking and law-preserving violence. Benjamin's problematisation has played an important role in the critical analysis of law and politics (see Butler 2006; Hamacher 1994; Martel 2014). This goes not the least for the discussion initiated by Jacques Derrida's (1992) reading of Benjamin.

Particularly important for the discussion of law in the context of Habermas' political and social thought is the analysis of the formative force of law among the early generation of Frankfurt theorists (see Buckel 2007: B.II; Scheuerman 1994: Chaps. 1–2; Seifert 1971). Kirchheimer (1928) and Franz Neumann (1937) engaged in the analysis of juridification, and they focused on the function of law in guaranteeing social and political status quo, its role in disguising social domination, but in particular understanding, how law has become central for framing conflicts and expressing claims. Kirchheimer (1928: 36f) discussed this in terms of the establishment of the modern idea of the 'legal state' (*Rechtsstaatsgedanke*) that is formative for modern politics. The legal state was initially a tool in the struggle of the bourgeoisie against both feudalism and absolutist monarchs and later became the framework of modern politics. It came to define the 'horizon' of politics, a shaping and forming effect that Kirchheimer found ambiguous for reasons similar to those articulated by Engels and Kautsky.

Habermas draws on Kirchheimer in *The Theory of Communicative Action*, when engaging in the analysis of how welfare state law is an example of the colonisation of the lifeworld. Kirchheimer, by contrast, addressed what Günther Teubner (1993) calls the 'colonisation' of politics, the formative role of law with regard to modern politics. Describing conflicts through modern law shapes the understanding of conflicts and the making of claims, what is possible to say and do. This simple fact directs attention to the kind of 'language' law is and what it makes possible to say. These features of what the force of law consists of are central to the modern critique of law (see Buckel 2009a; Christodoulidis 1998; Loick 2014b). Implied in Kirchheimer's criticism is, in the words of Emilios Christodoulidis (1998: 69), the critique that law serves 'as an (adequate) register of political meaning'. Yet, to talk about juridification as 'colonisation' of politics is in several ways imprecise; therefore, we have to engage in an analysis of the dialectic of law, how law is both a condition for freedom and a condition of social domination. As already discussed, the analysis of the dialectic of law involves stressing how the opposite of law, involving freedom or autonomy, is at the same time unfolding on the basis of law. In discussing this, I draw on Menke but there are other examples as well (compare Kompridis 2006). An example is Peter Fitzpatrick (2001) who argues that whereas modernity does not rely on some exteriority that defines it, it does produce the 'other' constitutive of it inside itself: 'Because a universalist encompassing modernity cannot allow of an engendering position apart from itself, its own 'self' creates the other against which it is constituted. Not only that, not only must the other be absolutely excluded from an encompassing modernity, this very quality of encompassment means that the other must also be included' (Fitzpatrick 2001: 63). Fitzpatrick analyses the conception of savagery in this context, how savagery is externally opposed to the civilisational role of law and yet included in it.

The Modern Legal Form

Important for the discussion of Habermas' conception of law in the light of the modern critique of law is the question about how to understand the modern legal form. As is discussed in more detail in the following two chapters, Habermas views modern legal forms partly in terms of system differentiation, that is, how law ties in with the development of the systems media of money and administrative power, partly in relation to lifeworld rationalisation. Both dimensions are important for Habermas' understanding of the law, but the lifeworld anchoring of law is a key to his understanding of modern legal forms.

The rationalisation of the lifeworld involves the differentiation of morality and legality. Compared to ancient understandings, neither morality nor law anchors in ethical life any longer. In discussing the implications of the rationalisation process that sets free values and norms and makes them depend on processes of coming to an understanding, the 'vanishing point' of these processes entails a situation in which 'legitimate orders are dependent upon formal procedures for positing and justifying norms' (Habermas 1981 [1987], vol. 2: 146). Thinking that both morality and legality evolve out of the disintegration of ethical life does not mean that Habermas, along the lines of Kant, thinks that morality is the basis of law. In the contrary, it is only democratic processes of lawmaking that constitute the source of legitimacy of laws. In fact, the differentiation of morality and law makes up an important background for the possibility of modern democracy. As noted in the previous chapter, Gaus (2013) argues that a key element to Habermas' reconstruction is that he thinks that citizens involved in establishing the constitution understand that they can only do so through positive law.

The key to the legal form for Habermas is how it involves a threefold abstraction in comparison with morality (see also Klein and Menke 2011). First, law abstracts from the capacity of persons to bind their own will, and it only relates to persons being capable of free choice or exercising free will (*Willkür*). Second, law abstracts 'the complexities that action plans owe to their lifeworld contexts', Habermas (1992 [1996]: 112) argues, and 'restricts itself to the *external relation* of interactive influence that typical social actors exert on one another'. Third, law abstracts the kinds of motivation that make persons abide by the law. Habermas (1992 [1996]: 112) argues that moral norms refer to persons individuated through their life histories, but it is different with legal norms:

> [L]egal norms regulate interpersonal relationships and conflicts between actors who recognize one another as consociates in an abstract community first produced by legal norms themselves. Although they, too, are addressed to individual subjects, these subjects are individuated not through personal identities developed over a lifetime but through the capacity to occupy the position of typical members of a legally constituted community.

Habermas (1992 [1996]: 112) argues that these characteristics of legal norms and the legal person make the legal form have an 'atomising effect', but this does not negate the intersubjective basis of law. By this, Habermas means, in ways that have certain affinities with Hegel's account, that the abstractions of the legal form and the notion of the person it contains do not compromise how law reflects the structures of recognition in communicative action (compare Buchwalter 2002; Stillman 1991).

While emphasising lifeworld rationalisation as important for law, Habermas also stresses the centrality of private law in the development of modern rights, rights tailored to individual choice. As Habermas (1992 [1996]: 27) notes, 'the core of modern law consists of private rights that mark out the legitimate scope of individual liberties and are thus tailored to the strategic pursuit of private interests'.[6] In line with the ambition to reconstruct the relationship between private and public autonomy, Habermas shifts from discussing how modern law involves stressing private autonomy to how this is a problem when we are interested in showing the interrelation of the two dimensions of autonomy. German civil law jurisprudence from Friedrich Carl von Savigny to Hans Kelsen, which is Habermas' focus in this discussion, 'concealed the real problem connected with the key position of private rights: the source from whence enacted law may draw its legitimacy is not successfully explained' (Habermas 1992 [1996]: 89).

Menke (2015) details the importance of private law for the modern form of rights in ways that Habermas does not. Unlike Habermas and several others, discussing modern legal forms in terms of abstraction, Menke puts less emphasis on this element. Central to Menke's analysis is instead how modern law builds on the relation between law and non-law. In this respect, his analysis resembles that of Luhmann but unlike Luhmann, Menke is not primarily interested in the sociological meaning of the normativity of modern law. Menke (2015: 7) focuses on understanding the specific form of equality institutionalised from the early modern revolutions onwards: equal rights. He develops on this in relation to Marx' (1843a [1992]: 230) puzzle regarding the French Revolution[7]:

> It is a curious thing that a people which is just beginning to free itself, to tear down all the barriers between the different sections of the people and to found a political community, that such a people should solemnly proclaim the rights of egoistic man, separated from his fellow men and from the community.

This, Marx thought, makes political freedom (the political community) into a means for realising rights manifested in private law. Menke thinks that the paradox of the early modern revolutions, political emancipation at the same time being an emancipation *from* politics, is understandable when investigating how this took place (compare Kouvélakis 2003). He suggests that understanding this 'how' requires us to look closer at the form it takes, the form of rights. Understanding Marx's puzzle necessitates investigating the form of rights and the modern legal form (Menke 2015: 7ff).

The key to Menke's (2013, 2015) conception of the modern legal form is that law relates to what is outside of it, to what is non-law (*Nichtrecht*). In its modern understanding, rights are about this relation to the outside of law in a twofold way. Rights relate to what is outside of law as the 'natural' striving to self-preservation, on the one hand, and the interiority of individuals, on the other hand. Thoughts, desires, and inclinations of individuals are outside of law, something that law cannot 'reach' or regulate. This means that modern law sets free thoughts and desires of individuals, allowing for their expression and development. Instead of trying to secure the ethical integration or education of individuals, their thoughts and inclinations are set free. Law only regulates external behaviour. As seen, Habermas shares this view, an understanding that is central to most philosophies of modern law. Famously, Kant (1797 [1991]: 56) conceptualised law in this way, as the 'sum of the conditions under which the choice of one can be united with the choice of another in accordance with a universal law of freedom'. Combing or regulating choices of individuals, as the latter are secured through rights are key to modern law. Moreover, these choices refer to the 'natural' striving for self-preservation. Self-preservation is about using powers and capacities for preserving and augmenting life. It is in this sense that Hobbes (1651 [1985]: Chap. 14 (189)) talked about the right of nature as the 'Liberty each man hath, to use his own power, as he will himself, for the preservation of his own Nature; that is to say, of his own Life'. The reference to what is outside of law is central for what the primacy of rights demands in modern law. Rights are about protecting the 'natural' striving, including the power and freedom this involves.

Both of these dimensions are important for understanding the primacy of rights in modern law. It is common to see the modern law as a change from duties to rights, following the dissolution of anchoring law in ethical life (Menke 1996). In much of modern natural law thinking, this shift to the primacy of rights means that rights exist prior to the establishing of the legal–political order. This, in turn, brings forward the counterclaim that only legally institutionalised rights are rights, properly speaking. Menke (2015: 28f) thinks that both interpretations misunderstand the implications of the modern focus on the primacy of rights. 'Natural rights' do not refer to the founding of law, rights existing prior to law and providing the ground for it but to the content of rights. It refers to the material of rights in that rights refer to what is outside of law. Rights are about mediating between law and the outside of law. Menke (2015: Chaps. 2–4) explicates this in relation to the understanding of rights as claims and the reasons for the following law.

Looking at the first dimension, rights as claims, Menke (2015: Chap. 2) points out that in Greek antiquity, rights were understood in terms of justice, in line with justice meaning 'to each his own'. Rights involved claims to what were due to persons on this basis. In settling claims, the focus was on restoring justice, what is properly due to persons. The Roman understanding was in some ways similar, that is, looking at legal claims in the light of what is just. However, in the Roman case, the equality of citizens was decisive in this regard, not the integration of citizens in a shared ethical life establishing what is good and worthwhile. Menke (2015: 47f and 90) interprets this as meaning that in Rome law was silent about the purposes of exercising rights. This is not the case in the modern understanding. The modern form of rights is not silent about the purposes of rights. Modern rights are about enabling individuals to engage in the natural striving for self-preservation. Thus, modern law is not only about the primacy of rights but also involves a specific understanding of what the legal claim is. It is a claim to something outside of law, to power or liberty to do something.

Concerning the second dimension, reasons for abiding by law, Menke (2015: Chap. 3) argues that in Greek antiquity, in line with seeing claims to what is one's own anchored in an order of what is good and worthwhile, law was about ethical education. Law was about making persons virtuous. The Roman conception differed from this because of the abstraction from ethical life. Self-preservation and virtue had the same ontological status. Developing virtue was one possibility, the natural striving for self-preservation another. Again, Menke argues that we should not confuse the modern and the Roman conceptions of law. While the modern understanding has certain similarities with the Roman understanding, characteristic of the modern form is how it allows for individual will and choice (*Willkür*). This allowing stems from modern law not being able to impose laws that run counter to the self-preservation of individuals. Menke (2015: 81ff) takes Hobbes' discussion of the sovereign as an example. Even though absolute and unlimited, the sovereign is restricted to the purpose of law, protecting self-preservation.

The sovereign cannot impose obligations that involve human beings acting against themselves, more specifically, against what is their own will. Menke (2015: 77ff) argues that this involves a turn to the interiority of individuals. Their will, which is the will for self-preservation, becomes central. This will is not uniform or 'simple' but dependent on the choice of individuals. Individuals use their own mind and imagination to make choices. Since self-preservation is their own concern, and rights are about enabling them in this natural striving, the sovereign cannot reach the inner thoughts of human beings. The latter are thereby set free.[8]

The combining of enabling self-preservation and allowing for individual choice that characterises modern law entails that both the activities for natural striving and the interiority of the individual are outside of law. Rights are about this dual relation to the outside of law, and modern law is characterised by this relation to non-law. The relation between law and non-law is key to the self-reflection of modern law, Menke (2011, 2015: Part 2) thinks. In this, he follows Luhmann's analysis of the structure of modern law. Modern law is 'law that reflects itself in its difference from its other, from that which is not law' (Menke 2011: 124). Yet, modern law also involves the stopping or denial of this reflection. Reflection is not fully carried through. The consequence is that the outside of law is viewed as 'given' (Menke 2015: Chap. 7).[9] This stopping or denial of self-reflection and the viewing of outside as given makes up the positivity or positivism of modern law. By positivism, Menke means the denial (*Verleugnung*) of reflection, as this has been criticised in epistemological discussions. Positivity is the term used by Hegel (1795) in understanding that which is handed down as given.

Menke argues that subjective rights express this positivity of modern law, the denial of carrying through the reflection between law and non-law. In this regard, we must pay attention to the distinction Menke makes between the concept of rights and its actual character in modern law. Conceptually, rights are about the carrying through of law's self-reflection regarding what is law and what is outside of law. Yet, actually existing modern law involves the denial of this self-reflection (Menke 2015: 164ff).[10] The actually existing law, in which subjective rights are central, is therefore opposite to the concept of rights. Conceptually, rights are the carrying through of reflection, but the actually existing law is instead the denial of this process. The outside of law appears as a result as given. This goes both for the outside in the sense of the capacities and powers involved in self-preservation and the interiority of individuals.

Menke's (2015: Chap. 7 and 13–15) argument that subjective rights express the denial of reflection implies that the critique of rights points to the need of setting free the process of reflection. This critique aims to continue the revolutionising of law and politics that began in the early modern era but which was only partially expressed in the eighteenth-century revolutions. Menke here relies on the familiar motif of Marx, who thought that the French Revolution stopped short of being full human emancipation and instead became the institutionalisation of bourgeois order. Marx looked upon the coming socialist revolution as fulfilling the revolutionising promise of modernity. However, Menke is at the same time critical of the implications of Marx' reasoning about the post-revolutionary society and develops an alternative reading by relying on Nietzsche. Menke (2015: Part 4) develops this in interesting ways, in this partly responding to Habermas' (2003) criticism of his earlier works.[11] However, I will not discuss this in more detail. The aim of this study is more modest, to reconsider some of the features of Habermas' elaboration of law and rights. For this purpose, I think that Menke's account of the modern legal form is useful.

Central in my view is how Menke discusses the primacy of rights in modern law, this referring to rights articulating a relationship to the outside of law. Similar to some reviewers, I am less convinced by Menke's analysis of the given (Möllers 2016). It seems to me that Menke gives two not always overlapping accounts of modern rights, one that involves the historical understanding of the primacy of rights and another that builds on subjective rights expressing the stopping and denial of self-reflection of law. The reason for thinking that these conceptions do not necessarily overlap is that there seem to be differences in how self-reflection is carried through and denied in the cases of private law liberalism and welfare state law. Certainly, both are modern legal paradigms, therefore, expressing an emphasis on rights related to individual will. However, they are different when we look at them from the point of view of reflection. The welfare state legal paradigm emerges out of criticism against private law liberalism. This criticism opens up for reflecting on what was given in private law liberalism, the reconsidering of assumptions about the relations between law and non-law. What is set free is a specific kind of denial of reflection found in private law liberalism. An expression of this is how it is central to welfare state law that the preconditions of freedom, education, and property, to speak with Marx, is taken into account when elaborating on equal rights and opportunities.

This does not mean that denial of reflection is absent from welfare state law, only that its shape is not the same as in the liberal paradigm of law. Thus, by arguing that actually existing law involves the denial of reflection, Menke underestimates the different shapes it takes in modern law. It does not seem to be the case that modern law is characterised by the same kind of denial of reflection. For this reason, I find his discussion of the denial of reflection somewhat problematic. However, this does not mean that Menke's historically oriented analysis of the primacy of rights and the modern form of rights is not both interesting and useful.

The relation-to-self that modern subjective rights enable is largely about the possibility of asserting one's own will. This assertion (or power) of the subject's will, Menke (2015: 207ff) argues, takes two forms in modern society. One of them involves demarcating a private sphere of the individual, a sphere in which the individual is free to do as he or she pleases. This is a common understanding of rights. Rights enable persons to make decisions, doing something or refraining from doing something. As already noted, this is what Kant expressed in his definition of law, and Habermas talks about private autonomy in similar ways. The conception of a private sphere is, however, only one of the relevant understandings in modern society. The other understanding is that which is central to the social law (and welfare state law).

Menke (2015: 207) illustrates this with the example of private property, which is the 'most simple and most fundamental' form of the legal enabling of the subject's will. Property played a key role in private law liberalism, not only for functional reasons but because it was an expression of the independence of persons, their will but also their work or labour. Several scholars point to the centrality of this, often discussed following C.B. Macpherson (1962) as 'possessive individualism'. Menke (2015: 211ff) argues that while this involves several paradoxes, notably the idea of persons 'owning' themselves as persons, what is decisive is the 'social' component of how will connects to work and labour. This element points beyond private law liberalism but was also contained in it, for instance, in how Locke understood property. For Locke, the subject of rights is not only the willing individual but also the working and labouring individual. What then comes into view are the capacities and knowledge that go into working and labouring. Abilities, knowledge and so on are central 'means' for making, creating, and cultivating matter. It is not only the individuals' will that counts but also his or her capacities and abilities. The latter are social in the sense that they are learned and mastered (or not) together with others (Menke 2015: 218ff).

Private law liberalism involved the regulation of these social dimensions through their private appropriation. Rights involved claims to this appropriation, the claim to call abilities 'mine', regulating the control over capacities by the individual. However, the social character of abilities and knowledge also means that built into this conception is the possibility of contesting the private law order. This takes the shape of stressing social partaking. This became important in several social movements from the nineteenth century onwards, even though it of course also resonates with a long tradition of stressing what is common. The focus on social partaking may take either of two forms. It may either involve an emphasis on partaking as an alternative to the private appropriation of capacities and abilities, or it may be stressing the equal access to the private appropriation of abilities and knowledge. When phrased in terms of rights, the latter dimension becomes central. This is largely how social partaking became institutionalised in welfare states. While being a transformation of liberal law, welfare state law is also similar to it in several respects. As Menke (2015: 223—my translation) states: 'The right of social partaking *follows* from the legal empowerment of the subject's own will…and that means are social and therefore only can be appropriated through partaking'. In this analysis, Menke stresses, similar to Habermas, the importance of private autonomy in private law liberalism (the liberal legal paradigm) and social law (the welfare state legal paradigm). The major difference between the thinkers is that Menke discusses this in terms of the private appropriation of socially developed capacities and abilities, whereas Habermas focuses on the social conditions for the exercise of individual liberties.

Menke's elaboration of the form of rights, rights relating to what is outside of law, has certain similarities with how other theorists address the importance of life when wanting to understand modern rights and modern law. Hannah Arendt (1958) pointed to this in her analysis of the centrality of labour and with that 'life itself', involving the emphasis of the biological dimension of human beings, as well as in her discussion of biological existence as problematic 'ground' of human rights (Arendt 1951: Chap. 9). Partly building on this, Foucault (1976a, b; 1978) developed an analysis of disciplinary and regulatory power in modern societies. Foucault (1976b: 142) makes the point that the partial shift from sovereign power to new forms of power in the eighteenth and nineteenth centuries implies that 'biological existence' for the first time 'was reflected in political existence'. In knowledge about individual bodies and populations, 'the fact of living was no longer an inaccessible substrate' but that which was actively engaged with, moulded and made part of the operations of power. This also implies a change in social and political struggles, in the nineteenth century increasingly focused on the right to life, rights concerning 'one's body, to health, to happiness, to the satisfaction of needs…was the political response to all these new procedures of power' (Foucault 1976b: 145).

Whereas Foucault did not focus primarily on law, law is central when discussing Giorgio Agamben (1995: 127), who directs attention to how the modern declarations of right 'represent the original figure of the inscription of natural life in the juridico-political order of the nation-state'. Agamben points in this regard to the inscription of the body, the *corpus*, in law, more specifically with regard to *habeas corpus* and the requirement to show the taken body. More generally, inscribed in modern rights and democracy is the understanding of life as *zoe*, the life that is common to living beings, human beings and animals alike, and not the qualified life of the citizen, the *bios*. Not *bios* but *zoe* came to define modern democracy. However, this inclusion of natural life has to be understood at the background of its exclusion in Greek antiquity. The result, Agamben (1995: 6) concludes, is the 'zone of indistinction' that defines the modern condition. Foucault (1976b) describes this process differently because life is not held in the sovereign ban. Menke's (2015: Chaps. 2–4) understanding of the modern legal form is closer to that of Foucault's than that of Agamben. The modern legal form is not the sovereign ban but instead the opening of law in relation to what is outside of law, rights playing the crucial role of articulating this relationship.

Conclusions

In this chapter, I have clarified the similarities and differences between analysing the dialectic of legal and factual equality, which Habermas focuses on in *Between Facts and Norms* and the dialectic of law. The latter refers to the law being simultaneously conditioned for emancipation and domination. Marx pointed to this in his discussion of legal equality and capitalist exploitation, and it guides Habermas' analysis of welfare state law as dilemmatic as such. Habermas later considers this characterisation as too rash and discusses instead the dialectic of legal and factual equality as a way of understanding the normalisation part of welfare state law. Habermas argues that the criteria for understanding when welfare state measures turn from promoting to restricting autonomy are given by the reconstruction of private and public autonomy. This implies that the problems of welfare state law arise because citizens are not able to take part in legislation, policy making, and so on, in proper ways. Habermas also relies on private autonomy independently of the reconstruction of private and public autonomy. This is not surprising, given the central role that private autonomy plays in modern law.

I have also addressed how to understand the modern legal form, contrasting Habermas' understanding of modern legal forms to that of Menke. Both authors stress the importance of private law and the understanding of private autonomy for the modern conceptualisation of rights. A major difference between them is that Habermas, similar to several other theorists, understands the legal form as an abstraction, whereas Menke argues that law is characterised by the relation between law and non-law, where rights have the central function of articulating this relation to what is outside of law. The modern form of rights is characterised by a twofold relation to the outside of law: it relating to the natural striving for self-preservation and to the interiority of individuals. The reason for discussing understandings of the modern law is that I think that Menke's characterisation of this form is of help in analysing the dialectic of law. I will specify this in the next chapter where I address Habermas' analysis in *The Theory of Communicative Action*. In my view, the latter analysis involves considering the dialectic of law but the way that Habermas does so, as the colonisation of the lifeworld, is problematic. Later, Habermas abandons this analysis but in doing so he also forfeits the analytical tools used to understand the dialectic of law. Instead, Habermas argues in *Between Facts and Norms* that normalisation in welfare state law is a side effect. This leaves us in a difficult situation because we cannot simply go back to the colonisation analysis when wanting to continue the analysis of the dialectic of law. We need other conceptual tools for this, and I suggest that Menke's analysis of the modern form of rights and the modern form of law is helpful in this regard.

Notes

1. As we will see in the following chapters, this makes up an important theme to Habermas' analysis of welfare state law, not only in *Between Facts and Norms* but also in *The Theory of Communicative Action*. It is

also evident in much of Habermas' previous works, for instance, when he analyses the public sphere in twentieth century welfare states (Habermas 1962) as well as in his discussions about technocracy (Habermas 1968). On the relation between these early discussions and the works of the 1980s and 1990s, see Specter (2010).

2. As is discussed in depth in Chap. 4, there is an extensive scholarly debate on these themes, broadly tying in with accounts of deliberative democracy and the role of social movements in modern democracies.
3. Coactus voluit means 'it is his wish, although coerced' (Weber 1922 [1978]: 752).
4. Habermas does not consider the objectives of Foucault's analysis of power, among them the shift away from the dominance of the juridical form of power in modern societies. Nor is he considering Foucault's argument that invoking right against discipline and normalisation is problematically tied to sovereignty (see Ashenden and Owen 1999). What is required, according to Foucault (1976a [2003]: 40), is a new type of right, 'both antidisciplinary and emancipated from the principle of sovereignty'. See also Buckel (2007: 198ff), Golder (2015), Mourad (2003), Tadros (1998).
5. Another example besides Habermas' critique of Foucault is his criticism of some of Menke's earlier arguments where the centre of attention is Menke arguing that there are limitations to liberal conceptions of equality that he thinks has bearings on the concept of equality as understood by liberals (more specifically, Rawls). Habermas (2003) argues against Menke's assessment by distinguishing between empirical analysis of the factual limitations to the realisation of equality and the conceptual clarification of equality.
6. Some scholars suggest that Habermas thereby underestimates the role of rights in protecting the possibilities of persons to develop their own conception of the good (compare Maus 1996: 850f). It is true that Habermas discusses this only marginally in *Between Facts and Norms,* but it makes up an important element to his discussion about cultural pluralism and multiculturalism (see Habermas 1996, 2003). Honneth (2011: B.I) engages in an extensive discussion of law and ethical self-examination. Legal freedom enables ethical self-examination, Honneth claims, but it is only half the story. The reason is that while the distancing from common sense is important for individuals figuring out what is their good life, the actual working out of what is good and worthwhile requires taking up relations to others. It is not possible for individuals to reflect on and to pursue what is good for themselves without relating to others in ways that include them as subjects that are like them engaged in developing and pursuing what is good. However, legal freedom does not secure this relation to others. In fact, legal freedom implies the distancing

from others in order to be free from social obligations. The result is paradoxical. Legal freedom guarantees freedom from common sense in order for individuals to be able to develop their own conception of the good, but cannot secure the conditions for this development to be possible.

7. Menke (2015: 7ff) notes that the phrase egoistic man is misleading, and one of the reasons for why Marx' point has often been misunderstood. Central in this regard is not the egoism as moral category but the private law conception of the individual.
8. As long as individuals follow law regarding the limitations it imposes on behaviour, the reason for following law is not the concern of law (Menke 2015: 78ff). As Habermas (1992: 47ff) notes regarding modern positive law, it leaves open the reason for obeying laws, either strategically, viewing laws as external obstacles, or out of respect of law.
9. Some reviewers think that Menke's account of the given and how to overcome it is unclear. For instance, Christoph Möllers (2016: 311—my translation) argues that Menke's analysis implies viewing 'law as deficient in so far that it is not politics'. For Möllers, law is inevitably implying an element of what is given because law is about stabilising relations, practices, and expectations.
10. Menke (2015: 165ff) uses the term 'bürgerlichen Recht' in this regard.
11. Habermas (2003 [2005]: 6) thought that Menke's reflections, the example here is his discussion of Rawls, express a certain 'quietism of a persistent reflection on the limits of freedom'. In *Between Facts and Norms*, Habermas (1992 [1996]: xlii) argues that he has no illusions about the problems of bringing out the 'hunch' he develops, that rule of law is only possible if combined with radical democracy, but that 'defeatism' is not justified.

References

Agamben, Giorgio. 1995 [1998]. *Homo Sacer. Sovereign Power and Bare Life*, trans. Daniel Heller-Roazen. Stanford: Stanford University Press.

Arendt, Hannah. 1951. *The Origins of Totalitarianism*. New York: Harcourt Brace.

Arendt, Hannah. 1958. *The Human Condition*. Chicago: University of Chicago Press.

Ashenden, Samantha, and David Owen (eds.). 1999. *Foucault Contra Habermas. Recasting the Dialogue Between Genealogy and Critical Theory*. London: Sage.

Balbus, Isaac. 1977. Commodity Form and Legal Form: An Essay on the "Relative Autonomy" of the Law. *Law & Society Review* 11 (3): 571–588.

Baynes, Kenneth. 2000. Rights as Critique and the Critique of Rights: Karl Marx, Wendy Brown, and the Social Function of Rights. *Political Theory* 28 (4): 451–468.

Benjamin, Walter (ed.). 1921 [1965]. Zur Kritik der Gewalt. In *Zur Kritik der Gewalt und andere Aufsätze*, ed. Herbert Marcuse, 29–65. Frankfurt: Suhrkamp.

Bourdieu, Pierre. 1987. The Force of Law: Toward a Sociology of the Juridical Field. *The Hastings Law Journal* 38: 805–853.

Brown, Wendy. 1995. *States of Injury. Power and Freedom in Late Modernity*. Princeton: Princeton University Press.

Brown, Wendy. 2000. Suffering the Paradoxes of Rights. *Constellations* 7 (2): 230–241.

Brown, Wendy, and Janet Halley (eds.). 2002. *Left Legalism/Left Critique*. Durham: Duke University Press.

Buchwalter, Andrew. 2002. Habermas, Hegel, and the Concept of Law. In *Discourse and Democracy. Essays on Habermas's Between Facts and Norms*, ed. René von Schomberg and Kenneth Baynes, 129–152. Albany: State University of New York Press.

Buckel, Sonja. 2007. *Subjektivierung und Kohäsion. Zur Rekonstruktion einer materialistischen Theorie des Rechts*. Weilerswist: Velbrück Wissenschaft.

Buckel, Sonja. 2009a. Zwischen Schutz und Maskerade – Kritik(en) des Rechts. *RAV Informationsbrief* 102: 11–23.

Buckel, Sonja. 2009b. Neo-Materialistische Rechtstheorie. In *Neue Theorien des Rechts*, ed. Sonja Buckel, Ralph Christensen, and Andreas Fischer-Lescano, 115–133. Stuttgart: Lucius & Lucius.

Butler, Judith. 1990. *Gender Trouble. Feminism and the Subversion of Identity*. New York: Routledge.

Butler, Judith. 2006. Critique, Violence, and Sacred Life in Benjamin's "Critique of Violence". In *Political Theologies. Public Religions in a Post-Secular World*, ed. Hent der Vries and Lawrence Sullivan, 201–219. New York: Fordham University Press.

Christodoulidis, Emilios. 1998. *Law and Reflexive Politics*. Dordrecht: Kluwer.

Collier, Richard. 1995. *Masculinity, Law and the Family*. London: Routledge.

Collins, Hugh. 1982. *Marxism and Law*. Oxford: Oxford University Press.

Derrida, Jacques. 1992. The "Mystical Foundation of Authority". In *Deconstruction and the Possibility of Justice*, ed. Drucilla Cornell, Michel Rosenfeld, and David Gray Carlson, 3–67. New York: Routledge.

Fine, Robert. 1984 [2002]. *Democracy and the Rule of Law. Marx's Critique of the Legal Form*. Caldwell, NJ: The Blackburn Press.

Fine, Robert. 2001. *Political Investigations. Hegel, Marx, Arendt*. Abingdon: Routledge.

Fine, Robert. 2013. Marxism and the Social Theory of Law. In *Law and Social Theory*, 2nd ed., ed. Reza Banakar and Max Travers, 95–110. Oxford: Hart.

Fitzpatrick, Peter. 2001. *Modernism and the Grounds of Law*. Cambridge: Cambridge University Press.

Foucault, Michel. 1976a [2003]. *Society Must Be Defended. Lectures at the Collège de France, 1975–1976*, trans. David Macey. New York: Picador.

Foucault, Michel. 1976b [1980]. *History of Sexuality. Vol. 1: An Introduction*, trans. Robert Hurley. New York: Vintage.

Foucault, Michel. 1978 [2007]. *Security, Territory, Population. Lectures at the Collège de France, 1977–1978*, trans. Graham Burchell. Houndmills: Palgrave.

Frankenberg, Günter. 2009. Partisanen der Rechtskritik: Critical Legal Studies etc. In *Neue Theorien des Rechts*, ed. Sonja Buckel, Ralph Christensen, and Andreas Fischer-Lescano, 93–111. Stuttgart: Lucius & Lucius.

Gaus, Daniel. 2013. Rational Reconstruction as a Method of Political Theory between Social Critique and Empirical Political Science. *Constellations* 20 (4): 553–570.

Golder, Ben. 2015. *Foucault and the Politics of Rights*. Stanford: Stanford University Press.

Habermas, Jürgen. 1962 [1990]. *Strukturwandel der Öffentlichkeit*. Frankfurt: Suhrkamp.

Habermas, Jürgen. 1963 [1988]. Naturrecht und Revolution. In *Theorie und Praxis*, ed. Jürgen Habermas, 89–127. Frankfurt: Suhrkamp. Translated by John Viertel as 'Natural Law and Revolution'. In Habermas, *Theory and Practice*. Boston: Beacon Press, 1973, pp. 82–120.

Habermas, Jürgen. 1968. *Technik und Wissenschaft als 'Ideologie'*. Frankfurt: Suhrkamp.

Habermas, Jürgen. 1981. *Theorie des kommunikativen Handelns*, 2 vols. Frankfurt: Suhrkamp. Translated by Thomas McCarthy as *The Theory of Communicative Action*, vol. 1 1984 and vol. 2 1987. Boston: Beacon Press.

Habermas, Jürgen. 1992 [1996]. *Faktizität und Geltung. Beiträge zur Diskurstheorie des Rechts und des demokratischen Rechtsstaats*. Frankfurt: Suhrkamp. Translated by William Rehg as *Between Facts and Norms. Contributions to a Discourse Theory of Law and Democracy*. Cambridge: Polity Press.

Habermas, Jürgen. 1996. Inklusion – Einbeziehen order Einschliessen? Zum Verhältnis von Nation, Rechtsstaat und Demokratie. In *Die Einbeziehung des Anderen. Studien zur politischen Theorie*, 154–184. Frankfurt: Suhrkamp.

Habermas, Jürgen. 2003 [2005]. Kulturelle Gleichbehandlung – und die Grenzen des Postmodernen Liberalismus. In *Zwischen Naturalismus und Religion. Philosophische Aufsätze*, ed. Jürgen Habermas, 279–323. Frankfurt: Suhrkamp. Translated as 'Equal Treatment of Cultures and the Limits of Postmodern Liberalism'. *The Journal of Political Philosophy*, vol. 13, no. 1: 1–28 (2005).

Hamacher, Werner. 1994. Afformative, Strike. Benjamin's "Critique of Violence". In *Walter Benjamin's Philosophy. Destruction and Experience*, ed. Andrew Benjamin and Peter Osborne, 110–138. Abingdon: Routledge.

Hegel, G.W.F. 1795 [1971]. Die Positivität der christlichen Religion. In *Frühe Schriften*, ed. Hegel, 104–216. Frankfurt: Suhrkamp.

Hobbes, Thomas. 1651 [1985]. *Leviathan*. ed. C.B. Macpherson. London: Penguin.

Honneth, Axel. 2011 [2014]. *Das Recht der Freiheit. Grundriss einer demokratischen Sittlichkeit*. Berlin: Suhrkamp. Translated by Joseph Ganahl as *Freedom's Right. The Social Foundations of Democratic Life*. Cambridge: Polity.

Hunt, Alan. 1985. The Ideology of Law: Advances and Problems in Recent Applications of the Concept of Ideology to the Analysis of Law. *Law and Society Review* 19 (1): 11–37.

Hutchinson, Allan, and Patrick Monahan. 1984. Law, Politics, and the Critical Legal Scholars: The Unfolding Drama of American Legal Thought. *Stanford Law Review* 36 (1/2): 199–245.

Johnson, Pauline. 2001. Distorted Communications. Feminism's Dispute with Habermas. *Philosophy and Social Criticism* 27 (1): 39–62.

Kant, Immanuel. 1797 [1991]. *Metaphysik der Sitten*, ed. Karl Vorländer. Hamburg: Felix Meiner Verlag, 1966. Translated by Mary Gregor as *The Methaphysics of Morals*. Cambridge: Cambridge University Press.

Kelley, Donald. 1978. The Metaphysics of Law: An Essay on the Very Young Marx. *The American Historical Review* 83 (2): 350–367.

Kennedy, Duncan. 1985. The Role of Law in Economic Thought: Essays on the Fetishism of Commodities. *The American University Law Review* 34: 939–1001.

Kennedy, Duncan. 2002. The Critique of Rights in Critical Legal Studies. In *Left Legalism/Left Critique*, ed. Wendy Brown and Janet Halley, 178–228. Durham: Duke University Press.

Kirchheimer, Otto. 1928 [1976]. Zur Staatslehre des Sozialismus und Bolschewismus. In *Von der Weimarer Republik zum Faschismus: Die Auflösung der demokratischen Rechtsordnung*, ed. Wolfgang Luthardt, 32–52. Frankfurt: Suhrkamp.

Klein, Eckart, and Christoph Menke (eds.). 2011. *Der Mensch als Person und Rechtsperson. Grundlage der Freiheit*. Berlin: Berliner Wissenschaftsverlag.

Kompridis, Nikolas. 2006. *Critique and Disclosure. Critical Theory between Past and Future*. Cambridge, MA: MIT Press.

Kouvélakis, Stathis. 2003. *Philosophy and Revolution. From Kant to Marx*, trans. G.M. Goshgarian. London: Verso.

Kress, Ken. 1989. Legal Indeterminacy. *California Law Review* 77 (2): 283–337.

Loick, Daniel. 2014a. Juridification and Politics: From the Dilemma of Juridification to the Paradoxes of Rights. *Philosophy and Social Criticism* 40 (8): 757–778.

Loick, Daniel. 2014b. Terribly Upright: The Young Hegel's Critique of Juridicism. *Philosophy and Social Criticism* 40 (10): 933–956.

Macpherson, C.B. 1962. *The Political Theory of Possessive Individualism: Hobbes to Locke*. Oxford: Clarendon Press.

MacKinnon, Catharine. 1989. *Toward a Feminist Theory of the State*. Cambridge, MA: Harvard University Press.

Martel, James. 2014. *The One and Only Law. Walter Benjamin and the Second Commandment*. Ann Arbor: University of Michigan Press.

Maus, Ingeborg. 1996. Liberties and Popular Sovereignty: On Jürgen Habermas's Reconstruction of the System of Rights. *Cardozo Law Review* 17 (4–5): 825–882.

Marx, Karl. 1843a [1992]. Zur Judenfrage. In *Marx-Engels Werke*, vol. 1, 347–377. Berlin: Dietz Verlag, 1977. Translated by Gregor Benton as 'On the Jewish Question'. In ed. Karl Marx, *Early Writings*, 211–242. London: Penguin.

Marx, Karl. 1843b [1977]. Kritik des Hegelschen Staatsrechts. In *Marx-Engels Werke*, vol. 1, 201–333. Berlin: Dietz Verlag.

Marx, Karl. 1867 [1992]. *Das Kapital. Kritik der politischen Ökonomie*. In *Marx-Engels Werke*, vol. 23. Berlin: Dietz Verlag, 1968. Translated by Ben Fowkes as *The Capital. A Critique of Political Economy*, vol. 1. Harmondsworth: Penguin.

Menke, Christoph. 1996. *Tragödie im Sittlichen. Gerechtigkeit und Freiheit nach Hegel*. Frankfurt: Suhrkamp.

Menke, Christoph. 2011. The Self-Reflection of Law and the Politics of Rights. *Constellations* 18 (2): 124–134.

Menke, Christoph. 2013. Die "andre Form" der Herrschaft. Marx' Kritik des Rechts. In *Nach Marx. Philosophie, Kritik, Praxis*, ed. Rahel Jaeggi and Daniel Loick, 273–295. Frankfurt: Suhrkamp.

Menke, Christoph. 2015. *Kritik der Rechte*. Berlin: Suhrkamp.

Möllers, Christoph. 2016. Form der Rechte als Form des Rechts? *Deutsche Zeitschrift für Philosophie* 64 (2): 307–312.

Mourad, Roger. 2003. After Foucault. A New form of Right. *Philosophy and Social Criticism* 29 (4): 451–481.

Neumann, Franz. 1937. Der Funktionswandel des Gesetzes im Recht der bürgerlichen Gesellschaft. In *Demokratischer und autoritärer Staat. Beiträge zur Soziologie der Politik*, ed. Franz Neumann, 7–57. Frankfurt: Suhrkamp.

Parla, Ayse. 2011. Undocumented Migrants and the Double Binds of Rights Claims. *Differences: A Journal of Feminist Cultural Studies* 22 (1): 64–89.

Pashukanis, Evgeny. 1924 [1989]. *The General Theory of Law and Marxism*, trans. Barbara Einhorn. London: Pluto Press.

Peters, Bernhard. 1991. *Rationalität, Recht und Gesellschaft*. Frankfurt: Suhrkamp.

Poulantzas, Nicos. 1978 [2000]. *State, Power and Socialism*, trans. Patrick Camiller. London: Verso.

Scheuerman, William. 1994. *Between the Norm and the Exception. Frankfurt School and the Rule of Law*. Cambridge, MA: MIT Press.

Seifert, Jürgen. 1971. Verrechtlichte Politik und die Dialektik der marxistischen Rechtstehorie. *Kritische Justiz* 4 (2): 185–200.

Specter, Matthew. 2010. *Habermas: An Intellectual Biography*. Cambridge: Cambridge University Press.

Stillman, Peter. 1991. Property, Contract, and Ethical Life in Hegel's *Philosophy of Right*. In *Hegel and Legal Theory*, ed. Drucilla Cornell, Michael Rosenfeld, and David Gray Carlson, 205–227. New York: Routledge.

Tadros, Victor. 1998. Between Governance and Discipline: The Law and Michel Foucault. *Oxford Journal of Legal Studies* 18 (1): 75–103.

Teubner, Gunther. 1993. "Man schritt auf allen Gebieten zur Verrechtlichung": rechtsoziologische Theorie im Werk Otto Kirchheimers. In *Der Einfluß deutschsprachiger Emigranten auf die Rechtsentwicklung in den USA und in Deutschland*, ed. Marcus Lutter, Ernst Stiefel, and Michael Hoeflich, 505–520. Tübingen: Mohr & Siebeck.

Tushnet, Mark. 1989. Rights: An Essay in Informal Political Theory. *Politics and Society* 17 (4): 403–451.

Unger, Roberto Mangabeira. 1986. *The Critical Legal Studies Movement*. Cambridge, MA: Harvard University Press.

Weber, Max. 1922 [1978]. *Wirtschaft und Gesellschaft. Grundriss der verstehenden Soziologie*, ed. Johannes Winckelmann. Tübingen: J.C.B Mohr, 1972. Translated by Ephraim Fischoff et al. as *Economy and Society. An Outline of Interpretive Sociology*. Edited by Guenther Roth and Claus Wittich. Berkeley: University of California Press.

CHAPTER 3

Colonisation of the Lifeworld and the Dilemma of Welfare State Law

Abstract This chapter addresses Habermas' analyses of law in *The Theory of Communicative Action*, in particular, the dilemmatic structure of welfare state law. Habermas discusses the dilemmatic structure of welfare state law as an example of the system colonisation of the lifeworld. Given the problems of the colonisation analysis, I suggest that there is a need for another way to address the dialectic of law. Taking my cue from Christoph Menke's analysis of the modern legal form, I discuss how this may be possible and what kinds of reconsiderations of Habermas' analysis this requires.

Keywords Welfare state law · Colonisation · Legal form · Habermas Menke

Introduction

Habermas conceptualises law as a hinge between system and lifeworld. Law is, therefore, central not only for understanding the repercussions of system media on the lifeworld but also for conceptualising how citizens can influence systems. The latter stands at the centre for the considerations in *Between Facts and Norms*, in which Habermas discusses how self-legislation by citizens is possible in modern functionally differentiated societies. As pointed out, in the latter work, Habermas argues that the dialectic of legal and factual equality, central to welfare states,

M. Spång, *Emancipation, Democracy and the Modern Critique of Law*, International Political Theory, DOI 10.1007/978-3-319-62890-5_3

has normalising side effects. However, these consequences do not affect Habermas' conclusion that law is language for autonomy because the reconstruction of private and public autonomy gives a standard for assessing when measures turn from promoting freedom to its opposite. The analysis in *The Theory of Communicative Action* is different. In elaborating on the colonisation of the lifeworld, Habermas (1981 [1987], vol. 2: 362) argues that the dilemma of the welfare state, since it both enables freedom and colonises the lifeworld, depends on characteristics of welfare state law:

> The negative effects of this – to date, final – wave of juridification do not appear as side effects; they result *from the form of juridification itself.* It is now the very means of guaranteeing freedom that endangers the freedom of the beneficiaries.

In the following, I discuss this interpretation of welfare state law in the background of Habermas' analysis of the relationships between lifeworld and system. Habermas (1986) later abandons the colonisation analysis. He does so for good reasons. However, the consequence is that the theme he addresses in *The Theory of Communicative Action*, how negative effects are intrinsic to the mode of guaranteeing freedom, disappears from view. As said, we cannot simply return to the colonisation analysis and therefore need to understand the dialectic of law in other ways. Menke's analysis of the modern legal form provides an alternative. Making use of this analysis requires reconsidering Habermas' account of the juridification waves of modern society and his analysis on normalisation in welfare state law. I attempt to show what this reconsideration involves in this chapter.

Lifeworld and System

In order to understand how law is hinged between lifeworld and system, we need to look closer at the meaning of the latter two concepts. Habermas' ambition in developing his two-tiered theory of modern society is to combine the phenomenological and the functional traditions in modern social theory and to revise Weber's account of modern rationalisation processes (see Benhabib 1986; Honneth 1985; Outhwaite 2009). Agreeing with Weber that the development of the capitalist economy and the bureaucratic state are central to modern societies, Habermas (1981, vol. 2: Chap. 5.2) argues that these developments build on what he calls the rationalisation of the lifeworld. Only at the background of the rationalisation of the lifeworld, was it possible for the systems media of money and administrative power to develop and take on structuring effects in modern societies.

The rationalisation of the lifeworld entails that traditions, norms and values, societal institutions and socialisation processes are set free from how they previously, in particular in archaic and traditional societies, were held together through religion and shared traditions and customs. These changes make communicative action, based on criticisable validity claims, central for social integration. More and more of social interactions depend on participants coming to understandings about the norms and values that should regulate their life together. The rationalisation of the lifeworld enables reflexive and more reasonable approaches to the design of institutions, how to address the validity of norms and values, and so on. Habermas (1981 [1987], vol. 2: 146) argues that less and less, the validity or legitimacy of norms and values 'go *back* to an ascribed normative consensus, but issue *from* the cooperative interpretation processes of participants themselves'.

This enlightenment process is, however, not without problems. The reproduction of social integration based on criticisable validity claims is fragile and instable. Communicative action cannot really carry the burden of social integration that falls to it in modern societies. Habermas (1992: 23f) argues in *Between Facts and Norms* that law relieves communicative action of some of this burden and that it does so without compromising communicative action. Modern law reflects the structures of recognition found in communicative action. In *The Theory of Communicative Action*, Habermas does not address law in this regard, but instead focuses on the role of system media in facilitating the material reproduction of modern societies. At the same time, system media also have negative effects. They shape the lifeworld in ways that in certain circumstances are damaging, thus, colonising it. Habermas theorises the repercussions of systems on the lifeworld as reification (colonisation) along the lines of the Marxian tradition of Lukács (1923) and Horkheimer and Adorno (1944/1947). Habermas (1981, vol. 2: Chap. 8) tries to develop his own version of the dialectic of enlightenment, centred on the thesis of the colonisation of the lifeworld (see also Habermas 1985: Chap. 12; Honneth 1985). System media can only develop based on a sufficiently rationalised lifeworld; however, these also have repercussions on the lifeworld, turning against it and colonising it. Habermas (1981 [1987], vol. 2: 155) calls this 'the irresistible irony of the world historical process of enlightenment':

> [T]he rationalization of the lifeworld makes possible a heightening of systemic complexity, which becomes so hypertrophied that it unleashes system imperatives that burst the capacity of the lifeworld they instrumentalize.

Communicative Action and Lifeworld Rationalisation

Habermas attempts to reformulate the diagnosis of the dialectic of enlightenment by anchoring reason in everyday, mundane practices in ways he thinks that the early Frankfurt theorists were not able to do. This failure explains, in Habermas' view, why Horkheimer and Adorno ended up equating the modern rationalisation of state and capitalism with rationalisation as such. Although the early critical theorists gestured to other understandings of reason, in line with their commitment to enlightenment, they could not account for its anchoring in everyday relations. Communicative action and the corollary concept of communicative rationality are supposed to provide ways out of this problem (Habermas 1981, vol. 1: Chap. 4 and vol. 2: Chaps. 6, 8; 1985: Chaps. 5 and 11–12).

Communicative action refers to coordination of action by way of reaching an understanding with somebody about something in the world. The success of communicative action depends on the mutual understanding between participants, for instance, how to interpret the situation in which action takes place, the purposes of action, common goals among participants, and so on. Communicative action differs from strategic action. The latter does not involve coming to an understanding with somebody about criticisable validity claims but the calculation by actors of how best to influence others in order to achieve goals. The relations to others and to the world differ between strategic and communicative action. For persons who act strategically, 'all situational features are transformed into facts they evaluate in the light of their own preferences', Habermas (1992 [1996]: 27) argues, 'whereas actors oriented toward reaching understanding rely on a jointly negotiated understanding of the situation and interpret the relevant facts in the light of intersubjectively recognized validity claims'.

Communicative action involves making validity claims about the truth of statements, the sincerity of speakers, and the normative rightness of norms and values. We 'always already' make such claims. They are unavoidable presuppositions in linguistically mediated interaction (Habermas 1981: vol. 1: Chaps. 1 and 3, 1986, 1992: Chap. 1; see also Cooke 1994). In everyday interaction, claims remain uncontested most of the time. However, participants can challenge and criticise these validity claims. They then ask for reasons, for instance, why something is true or why a certain norm is the right one, appropriate in this context, and so on. When discussing validity claims, participants shift from communicative action, where the focus lies on coordinating action, to the discussion about reasons for and against the validity of claims. When individuals engage in this kind of conversation, which Habermas calls discourse, validity claims are the explicit focus of the discussion.[1] Discourse plays a central role in understanding the 'politicisation' of everyday interaction and its connection to institutionalised politics. The contestation of validity claims allows for what Habermas (1991) calls 'transcendence from within', the possibility of transforming values and norms as well as their institutional embodiments.[2]

The lifeworld is a corollary concept of communicative action. When persons communicate with each other and coordinate their actions through communication, they do so in the background of the lifeworld. In most everyday cases of communicative action, participants do not contest the validity of what others say but remain focused on the coordination of action. The validity of claims is naively accepted and remains in the background. It makes up 'common sense', which consists of interpretations, pre-understandings, and taken for granted knowledge. Besides this common sense, the lifeworld also consists of membership in social groups and personal identities. When communicating with each other, individuals generate and regenerate their belonging to social groups and forms of solidarity.[3]

The rationalisation of the lifeworld involves the gradual uncoupling of norms and values central for institutional complexes from comprehensive worldviews. Habermas (1981, vol. 2: Chap. 5.3) discusses this as processes of the linguistification (*Versprachlichung*) of the sacred. In premodern societies, the authority of the sacred held together cultural traditions and provided the legitimacy of norms and values.[4] In the course of societal evolution, traditions, norms and values become more and more open to interpretation. These interpretations follow from participants taking stances towards criticisable validity claims. Habermas (1981 [1987], vol. 2: 77) argues that the legitimacy of norms and values are thus made dependent on processes of coming to an understanding about the validity of them and 'the authority of the holy is gradually replaced by the authority of an achieved consensus'. He further contends that the spellbinding power of the sacred becomes 'the binding/bonding force of criticizable validity claims' (Habermas 1981 [1987], vol. 2: 77, emphasis deleted). The rationalisation of the lifeworld plays an important role in Habermas' analysis of law, as pointed out in the Introduction. Modern law both relieve communicative action of the burden of carrying social integration it cannot really bear and is itself an expression of this rationalisation, as modern law no longer build on the sacred or is anchored in ethical life.

Systems and the Colonisation of the Lifeworld

Habermas (1981, vol. 2: Chap. 7) relies on Parsons' elaboration on system differentiation in accounting for the functional differentiation of modern societies.[5] Habermas argues that in the course of social evolution, the complexity of systems grows, as does the rationality of the lifeworld. Moreover, there is an increasing differentiation between lifeworld and system media, which in modern societies leads to a partial uncoupling of them. The result, according to Habermas (1981 [1987], vol. 2: 154), is that:

> [M]odern societies attain a level of system differentiation at which increasingly autonomous organizations are connected with one another via delinguistified media of communication: these systemic mechanisms – for example, money – steer a social intercourse that has been largely disconnected from norms and values, above all in those subsystems of purposive rational economic and administrative action that, on Weber's diagnosis, have become independent of their moral-political foundations.

With the concept of systems media, Habermas wants to capture the kind of social objectivity that political economists and sociologists thought was central for understanding modern societies and to connect this to the critical analysis of how system colonises the lifeworld. In this regard, Habermas distinguishes between system media and natural languages used in communicative action. Systems media are generalised media of communication, which transmit highly specific information, for instance, as prices transmit information about demand and supply between producers and consumers. System media 'simulate' some of the features of natural languages, but also differ from them. Most importantly, system media does not reproduce 'the internal structure of mutual understanding which terminates in the recognition of criticizable validity claims and is embedded in a lifeworld context' (Habermas 1981 [1987], vol. 2: 263).

This difference between natural languages and system media is central for Habermas because it both explains why system media enables highly complex forms of integration across vast spaces, such as world markets, and makes understandable why system integration may be a problem. Problems appear when system media replaces coming to an understanding about norms and values. Integration then no longer takes place through criticisable validity claims, but through 'functional interconnections that are not intended' by participants, and usually, these interconnections are 'not even perceived within the horizon of everyday practice' (Habermas 1981 [1987], vol. 2: 150). In this way, Habermas tries to reformulate Marx' analysis of 'real abstraction' and the analysis of reification formulated by Lukács, the early Frankfurt theorists and Alfred Sohn-Rethel (1972). While system media has rationalising effects because they contribute to more efficient economic production and the more effective realisation of collective goals, they also have repercussions on the lifeworld, under certain conditions colonising it. Habermas (1981 [1987], vol. 2: 186) argues that 'The rationalization of the lifeworld makes possible the emergence and growth of subsystems whose independent imperatives turn back destructively upon the lifeworld itself'.

Whereas communicative action involves coordinating action via the working out of action orientations, system media 'reaches right through' orientations for action, as expressed by Habermas (1981 [1987], vol. 2: 150). The primary example of the latter is markets. By 'reaching right through' action orientations, system media shapes what people do and how they interact with others by circumventing processes of coming to an understanding about value orientations. What reaches right through may not appear for individuals as structuring what they do, or it may appear as inevitable and unavoidable. The socio-economic and political systems that participants are part of then appear as orders separate from their practices, as standing above and against them. As Habermas (1981 [1987], vol. 2: 154) puts it:

> Members behave toward formally organized action systems, steered via processes of exchange and power, as toward a block of quasi-natural reality; within these media-steered subsystems society congeals into a second nature.

While relying on the Marxian account of real abstraction, Habermas is also critical of Marx' understanding of system differentiation and reification. According to Habermas (1981 [1987], vol. 2: 339), Marx failed to understand that the destruction of feudalism meant 'a higher level of system differentiation, which simultaneously opens up new steering possibilities *and* forces a reorganization of the old, feudal, class relationships'. However, this contrast is largely misleading since Marx, like Smith and Hegel before him, thought that capitalism was a more advanced form of production compared to feudalism. Habermas also criticises Marx for lacking criteria in distinguishing between the reification of post-traditional forms of life—forms of life based on the modern symbolic structure of the lifeworld—and the destruction of life forms that do not exhibit this symbolic structure. This is a contestable interpretation but disregarding this, we may ask if Habermas fares better in articulating criteria that allow him to distinguish between colonisation and destruction of forms of life more generally. Habermas' (1981 [1987], vol. 2: 261) basic contention is that 'the only functional domains that can be differentiated out of the lifeworld by steering media are those of material reproduction. The symbolic structures of the lifeworld can be reproduced only via the basic medium of communicative action'. From this follows that colonising effects arise when system media replace or significantly affect the symbolic reproduction of the lifeworld:

> The conversion to another mechanism of action coordination, and thereby to another principle of sociation, results in reification...only when the lifeworld cannot be withdrawn from the functions in question, when these functions cannot be painlessly transferred to media-steered systems of action. (Habermas 1981 [1987], vol. 2: 375)

This suggests that the criterion for colonisation relies on the distinction between material and symbolic dimensions of reproduction (compare Cook 2006). Both this suggestion and, in particular, how Habermas maps the lifeworld-system distinction onto institutions and spheres of society have been much criticised (see Baxter 2011: 45ff;

Honneth 1985: Chap. 8; McCarthy 1985; Peters 1994). As Baxter (2011: 50) states, Habermas shifts from viewing the lifeworld as context for and resource in interaction to 'a conception of the lifeworld as itself a *domain of action*' that stands opposed to 'media-steered spheres of action'. Habermas often writes as if certain institutions are primarily about system integration, whereas other institutions are sites of social integration. This leads to several problems, as pointed out by critics. Besides failing to take seriously that the distinction is analytical and that lifeworld and systems cannot demarcate domains or institutions, it also underestimates that processes of coming to an understanding on criticisable validity claims do play roles also in corporations and state administrations. Interaction in these institutions is hardly 'norm-free', as Habermas sometimes suggests (see Baxter 2011: 33ff; Jütten 2013; McCarthy 1985; Peters 1994). Moreover, sites of social integration, for instance, families are imbued with power that in various ways are linked with system media (Fraser 1990: Chap. 6; see also Loick 2014).

Habermas (1986) later acknowledges that he was somewhat unclear on these issues and that the expression 'norm-free sociality' when talking about systems invited misunderstandings. Habermas clarifies that he did not want to deny that communicative action plays a role in corporations and state bureaucracies, only that they, in the final instance, are not based on social integration through communicative action.[6] He also underlines that he by no means intended to suggest that the lifeworld is free of power. To the contrary, social integration often takes place in the context of domination.[7]

A further complication in the discussion of criteria for assessing colonising effects is the question of whether they change over time. Habermas is not particularly clear on this point. Some parts of his discussion suggest that Marx was right in understanding capitalism in the early and mid-nineteenth century as involving colonisation effects but that it would wrong to understand mid and late twentieth century capitalism in these terms. For Habermas, the institutionalisation of collective bargaining, labour laws, and social rights in welfare states means that social pathologies are no longer class specific (Habermas 1981, vol. 2: Chap. 8.2). Irrespective of how we understand the value of this diagnosis, for instance, it being more plausible during the heydays of the Keynesian welfare state than in the contemporary context of neoliberalism, it does suggest that criteria for colonisation are historically variable. As Timo Jütten (2011: 714) recently points out, this means that 'the possibility of differentiating out the material reproduction of society without reification effects is the contingent result of the welfare state compromise'.

The colonisation analysis attempts to capture the transformations that take place through the uncoupling of systems and lifeworld in modern societies. This uncoupling is, however, only partial because system media remain anchored in the lifeworld. Morality and law play central roles in this regard because they are 'specifically tailored to check open conflict in such a way that the basis of communicative action—and with it the social integration of the lifeworld —does not fall apart', as noted by Habermas (1981 [1987], vol. 2: 173). Following Durkheim, Habermas argues that both morality and law in the course of societal evolution have become more abstract and universal. The increasingly abstract and universal character of both law and morality plays an important role in Habermas' discussion of modern legal orders.

Looking at law in modern societies more specifically, Habermas notes that the emergence of the separation of private and public law is important in the transition from feudal to modern societies:

> Whereas civil society is institutionalized as a sphere of legally domesticated, incessant competition between strategically acting private persons, the organs of state, organized by means of public law, constitute the level on which consensus can be restored in cases of stubborn conflict. (Habermas 1981 [1987], vol. 2: 178)

In this regard, the question of how to understand the interrelation of lifeworld and system becomes central. Habermas (1981 [1987], vol. 2: 187) argues that we could not infer any 'linear dependency in one direction or the other' from the uncoupling of lifeworld and system. Institutions may serve to channel influence of the lifeworld on system media, or the opposite, they may channel influence of systems on the lifeworld. Thus, Habermas understands law in a dual sense. Since system media anchors in the lifeworld through law, law allows for 'tracking' the colonisation of the lifeworld. This is central to Habermas' analysis of the dilemma of the welfare state. However, law is also of importance for understanding how citizens may influence the regulation of system media based on lifeworld orientations. These two perspectives on law follow from Habermas' conception of law as 'hinge' between lifeworld and system (see also Baxter 2011: 152f).

Legality and Legitimacy

Habermas (1981, vol. 2: 259ff) argues that the development of law (and morality) from archaic to modern societies allows for understanding changes of social integration. The rationalisation of the lifeworld entails that the legitimation of legal and political institutions and comprehensive worldviews are disconnected. Habermas draws on Durkheim in discussing the transition from spellbound authority of the sacred to modern ideas of binding authority and on Weber for addressing the intertwining of law and societal rationalisation.

Habermas agrees with Weber that several of the features of modern law, for instance, its positivity and formalism, link together with the development of the bureaucratic state and the capitalist economy. However, the functional fit of law, markets, and state do not fully explain modern legal structures. Habermas (1981 [1984], vol. 1: 261) argues that the domain of legality 'stands in need of practical justification' and continues:

> The particular accomplishment of the positivization of the legal order consists in *displacing* problems of justification, that is, in relieving the technical administration of the law of such problems over broad expanses – but not in doing away with them.

Habermas thinks that Weber did not capture this displacing but instead understood the positive law to imply the doing away with the need for legitimation of the legal system. The belief in legality that Weber stressed is insufficient for understanding legitimacy. Habermas (1981 [1984], vol. 1: 265) contends that this belief 'can produce legitimacy only if we already presuppose the legitimacy of the legal order that lays down what is legal', Habermas (1981 [1984], vol. 1: 263) argues that Weber constructed an

> antithesis between modern law in the strict sense, which rests only on the principle of enactment, and the not yet completely "formal" law of modern natural law theories which rests upon principles of grounding (however rational). In his view, modern law is to be understood in a positivistic sense, as law that is enacted by decision and fully disconnected from rational agreement, from ideas of grounding in general, however formal they might be (emphasis deleted).

Habermas contends that this relates to the failure of Weber to properly understand the implications of modern natural law. Weber conflated procedural conditions for the legitimation of law with the legitimation of law through substantial (material) values (compare Eder 1978).

The failure to understand the accomplishment of modern natural law led Weber to misunderstand the forms of legal structures. We cannot explain 'the forms of modern law', Habermas (1981 [1984], vol. 1: 260) argues, solely with reference to the modern state and the modern capitalist economy. Modern law also expresses the rationalisation of the lifeworld and 'post-traditional structures of moral consciousness' (Habermas 1981 [1984], vol. 1: 260). By the latter, Habermas has in mind post-conventional modes of justifying norms and values. Norms and values are justified in these modes with reference to universal principles that invite and require reflexive stances by participants (see Apel 1988; Habermas 1981, vol. 2: 259ff; Kohlberg 1981). Modern law thus expresses evolutionary features of lifeworld rationalisation, and this analysis plays an important role in Habermas' account of the waves of juridification central for the modern state. This is also the basis for the discussion about law in *Between Facts and Norms* where the articulation of the procedural conception of law and reason found in modern natural law plays an important role in the account of the connection between positive law and democratic legitimacy (see Niesen and Eberl 2009).

Juridification and the Ambivalence of Law

Law is pacemaker in the development from archaic to modern societies, through which Habermas tracks the rationalisation of the lifeworld. Law is also pacemaker in a second sense, with regard to system differentiation and the anchoring of systems in the lifeworld, which Habermas (1981, vol. 2: 522ff) discusses in terms of the juridification waves of modern societies, from the bourgeois state to the welfare state. Habermas' analysis of juridification is an attempt to show how law as a hinge between lifeworld and system involves both system media influencing the lifeworld and vice versa.

The first juridification wave, establishing the bourgeois state, took place during the transition from feudal to modern societies. It encompassed the modern combination of the capitalist economic order and the sovereign state, manifested in private law, built around the freedom of contract and private property, and in public law through designating the sovereign as source of legal authority. Habermas (1981 [1987]: vol. 2: 358) notes:

> On the one hand, relations among individual commodity owners were subjected to legal regulation in a code of civil law tailored to strategically acting legal persons who entered into contracts with one another. /—/On the other hand, public law authorizes a sovereign state power with a monopoly on coercive force as the sole source of legal authority.

Habermas analyses the bourgeois state primarily in system terms, as the institutionalisation of the modern capitalist economy and as the institutionalisation of an administrative apparatus. To a certain extent, this process entails the pushing aside of the lifeworld, which, however, plays a key role in the subsequent juridification waves. Habermas (1981 [1987], vol. 2: 359) contends that in fact, the latter waves can all 'be understood in these terms: a lifeworld that at first was placed at the disposal of the market and of absolutist rule little by little makes good its claims'. Both the constitutional and the constitutional-democratic state are examples.

In the constitutional state, which develops in the seventeenth and the eighteenth centuries, Habermas (1981 [1987], vol. 2: 359) argues that 'the bourgeois order of private law is coordinated with the apparatus for exercising political rule in such a way that the principle of the legal form of administration can be interpreted in the sense of the "rule of law"'. The important step accomplished through the constitutional state is that the guarantees of life, liberty, and property are no longer simply side effects of a 'commerce institutionalized in civil law' (Habermas 1981 [1987], vol. 2: 360). To be sure, private ordering remained central, but the guarantees of life, liberty, and property achieved 'the status of morally justified constitutional norms' in the constitutional state, which therefore also can be seen as inaugurating the basic mode of legitimacy in the modern state: Habermas (1981 [1987], vol. 2: 360) concludes that it is 'legitimation *on the basis* of a modern lifeworld' In the third wave, the legitimation of laws are tied to the participation of citizens in politics, and the two principles of human rights and popular sovereignty became the basis for the legitimacy of the legal order as such.

The juridification waves from the bourgeois state to the constitutional-democratic state show how modern juridification processes relate to both lifeworld rationalisation and system differentiation. Both are central to modern law. However, we may ask if this properly addresses the specificity of the modern legal form and the modern form of rights. Menke's (2015) analysis of the modern legal form is helpful in shedding light on features of the modern legal form that Habermas does not stress. Habermas' discussion of Hobbes is instructive in this regard. Habermas (1981 [1987], vol. 2: 358) argues that Hobbes expressed the 'self-understanding' of the age in the 'most consistent' way but that he also misunderstood modern law because he did not understand the structures of the modern lifeworld. According to Habermas (1981 [1987], vol. 2: 358), Hobbes defined 'the lifeworld negatively—it encompasses everything excluded from the administrative system and left to private discretion'. This requires that everything that is 'not constituted in the forms of modern law must appear *formless*' (Habermas 1981 [1987], vol. 2: 359). For Habermas, Hobbes was unable to see how the release from feudal structures and traditional forms of life entails and corresponds with lifeworld rationalisation. Hobbes did not properly represent the underlying rationalisation of the lifeworld and the development of post-traditional approaches to questions about the validity of norms and values. This charge against Hobbes plays an important role in Habermas' argument that the subsequent juridification waves after the initial establishment of the bourgeois state make good the claims of the lifeworld.

We may look at this in a different way and stress how Hobbes articulated certain key features of the modern legal form. Following Menke's (2015: Chap. 5) interpretation of Hobbes, the formless of the lifeworld is due to the specificity of the legal form, not the inadequate reflection of the rationalisation of the lifeworld. The modern conception of rights, rights relating to what is outside of law, entails that non-law is formless. As Menke (2015: 135—my translation) notes: 'Law is the form; non-law (*Nichtrecht*) is—relative to the form of law—the formless'. By designating what is outside of law as formless, Hobbes formulated a characteristic of modern law. This is one of the differences between the interpretations of Menke and that of Habermas. For Menke, the formlessness of what is outside of law is central feature of modern law because rights are about this relation between non-law and law. For Habermas, in contrast, it is misunderstanding of how law connects to the rationalisation of the lifeworld. Habermas therefore considers Hobbes to be concerned with law from a systems perspective, the institutionalisation of the modern market economy, and administrative power.

In the context of this study, the importance of Menke's interpretation lies in us being able to analyse the dialectic of law without relying on the system-lifeworld distinction. Habermas interprets modern law through these concepts and his account of welfare state juridification as dilemmatic builds on it, as discussed below. Given the problems of the analysis of the colonisation of the lifeworld, it is important to base the account of the dialectic of law on another conceptualisation of modern law. Suggested here is that Menke's account of the modern legal form provides for this. Taking up Menke's account does not imply that we cannot understand modern law in terms of the rationalisation of the lifeworld. However, it does mean that this rationalisation process does not capture specific features about the modern legal form. The relation between law and non-law is key to the normativity of modern law. The outside is formless when viewed from the point of view of the legal form. The forming of this outside of law takes place through law, more specifically as rights.

Juridification and Colonisation of the Lifeworld

Habermas claims that whereas the constitutional and constitutional-democratic juridification waves are unequivocally freedom-guaranteeing phases of juridification, neither the bourgeois state nor the welfare state is. The difference between these two phases is that while problems relating to the bourgeois state were side effects of private law, the dilemmatic structure of the welfare state relates inherently to the mode of administrative-legal provisions of social rights and interventions in personal life.

Welfare states facilitate freedom, institutionalise more equal opportunities for persons, and aim at restructuring social and economic conditions, although to varying degrees. However, the welfare state also has adverse effects, making welfare state law dilemmatic. Habermas (1981, vol. 2: 531ff) points to a couple of characteristics in this regard. Individualisation of entitlements restructures relations between persons in ways that enhance their freedom but also adversely affect relations between family members, relatives, friends, and so on. The bureaucratic implementation of welfare state measures entails the interpretation of situations and needs in standard ways, which has normalising effects. Moreover, the bureaucratic mode of implementation marginalises the participation of persons. Defined as clients rather than citizens, they have few opportunities to influence the provision of services. Welfare state provisions often take the form of monetary compensation of risks, which largely redefines lifeworld problems in consumerist ways. Habermas adds a fourth feature to this: therapeutic assistance, which is ambivalent because while it aims to promote the independence of clients, it takes the shape of experts using specific forms of knowledge for correcting and redefining individual behaviour (see also Kübler 1985; Teubner 1988).

It is not entirely clear why juridification results in the colonisation of the lifeworld only at the stage of the welfare state (see also Blichner and Molander 2008). Habermas discusses three criteria. One of these concerns the distinction between liberties and participation rights, sometimes invoked by liberal authors. Habermas (1981, vol. 2: 535ff) argues that this interpretation is not convincing and considers a second interpretation, which centres on the delinking of legality and legitimacy. This is the problem of legal positivism, that is, the legitimation of laws only by reference to enactment of laws and not to their substantial justification. The latter may suggest addressing laws in terms of substantial criteria of justice, for instance, as formulated by Rawls; however, what Habermas has in mind with substantial justification is the discursive legitimation of law. In line with the argument that modern natural law articulates a procedural account of reason, justification of laws involves discourses in which participants are free and equal partners, where they can address the validity claims raised, discuss reasons, and so on. As will be discussed in the next chapter, Habermas later develops on these elements in relation to the democratic circulation of power from the periphery of publics and civil society to the centre of parliaments, government, and other political bodies. In *The Theory of Communicative Action*, Habermas had not yet developed this account of democracy, even though elements of it were already present in his discussions of the ideal speech situation and its implications for questions about legitimacy (see also Habermas 1973: Part 3).

In *The Theory of Communicative Action*, Habermas discusses the distinction between law as medium and law as institution in this context (see Scheuerman 2013). Law as institution means that laws remain tied to substantive justification and legitimation. This is not the case with law as medium, which means the enacting of laws only with reference to the correct procedure. Moreover, law as medium connotes that law has become a steering medium, which occurs when 'law is combined with the media of power and money in such a way that it takes on the role of a steering medium itself' (Habermas 1981 [1987], vol. 2: 365).[8] Thus, law as a steering medium builds on two features, the positivistic understanding of legitimation and the assimilation of law and system media. This is, however, not by itself sufficient for talking about colonisation. Colonisation effects arise only when regulating relations that are not yet formally organised[9]:

> As a medium, social welfare law is tailored to domains of action that are first constituted in legal forms of organization and that can be held together only by systemic mechanisms. At the same time, however, social welfare law applies to situations embedded in informal lifeworld contexts. (Habermas (1981 [1987], vol. 2: 367)

Habermas (1981 [1987], vol. 2: 367) advances the interpretation that the dilemmatic structure of the welfare state becomes evident because it 'regulates exigencies that, as lifeworld situations, belong to a communicatively structured area of action'. This analysis builds on his discussion of the criteria of colonisation addressed previously in this chapter and suffers for this reason from similar weaknesses, that is, problems with the distinction between material and symbolic reproduction and the mapping of the lifeworld-system distinction onto specific institutions and spheres.[10]

The regulation of exigencies of the lifeworld in the welfare state means that domains dependent on social integration through processes of coming to an understanding are converted through 'the steering medium of the law, to a principle of sociation that is, for them, dysfunctional' (Habermas 1981 [1987], vol. 2: 373). This conversion is not simply one of 'abstracting' from lifeworld contexts. However, some scholars, for example, William Scheuerman (2013), argue that Habermas thinks that the problem of the welfare state is one of how law abstracts from lifeworld contexts. While it is true that Habermas (1981 [1987], vol. 2: 363) talks about the 'violent abstraction' from lifeworld contexts involved in welfare state law, this abstraction primarily refers to 'standard interpretations' of needs and action situations in bureaucratic provisions of services and the like. The brunt of the analysis does not depend on law involving 'abstraction', though, but the normalising consequences of welfare state law. As stressed, Habermas analyses this in terms of system colonisation. The key in this respect is how system media reaches right through action orientations. It is the circumventing of action orientations that is central for reification. Reification means that societal integration takes place behind the back of participants. To them, it may appear as necessary and inevitable, how ‘things are’. Societal relations are reified when they appear as given. For this reason, reification is not simply the abstraction from lifeworld contexts. In my view, Scheuerman (2013: 575) disregards the latter important point, arguing that in ‘Habermas’ narrative, the intrusion of abstract formal law was culpable for legal pathologies resulting from the colonization of the lifeworld: the abstract media of power and money joined arms with formal law, resulting in worrisome “violent abstractions”’.

I think that Scheuerman misses important points about Habermas' account of system repercussions and reification and disregards how Habermas addresses the welfare state as largely involving the materialisation of law, not formal abstract law. It is only by disregarding this that Scheuerman (2013: 575) can argue that Habermas' analysis ‘implicitly reproduced elements of the troublesome orthodox Marxist view that general or formal law was seamlessly welded to the commodity form’. Besides this reproach misunderstanding of how law as medium is tied to the account of reification not as a matter of abstraction but as colonisation, it also disregards how Habermas does not tie welfare state law directly to the commodity form. On the contrary, central to the analysis of the welfare state is that it changes how lifeworld and the money-steered economy relate to each other. As discussed above in relation to Jütten's elaboration of colonisation, the welfare state significantly changed the relation between the capitalist economy and the lifeworld.

While this argument in relation to Scheuerman's interpretation, in my view, points out that Habermas' interpretation of colonisation through the welfare state is more sophisticated than sometimes argued, in the end, the criteria suggested for colonisation are either unclear or not convincing. Most troubling is the mapping of analytical distinctions to domains noted by critics (see Deflem 2013; Eder 1988). Yet, what Habermas attempts to diagnose is at the same time important. The normalisation built into the welfare state is pervasive and underlines the dialectic of law, how in this case the rights to take part in social life connect to normalisation. In so far, Habermas is correct to point to the paradoxes of welfare state law, that is, it both enables freedom and is a condition for social domination. Moreover, he is right in pointing out that this kind of social domination is not class specific, even though effects are class related (see Scheuerman 2013).

Habermas (1992: Chap. 9) later abandons his analysis of welfare state law and argues that it was too rash to characterise the welfare state as inherently dilemmatic. In *Between Facts and Norms*, he looks at the welfare state in terms similar to his analysis of the bourgeois state, specifically, it has troubling side effects. Habermas (1992: Chap. 9) argues that the liberal and the welfare state paradigms of law are problematic because they both fail to take seriously the underlying premise of the democratic state: citizens being authors of law. Habermas advances this claim in *The Theory of Communicative Action* as well, although articulated less systematically. Besides the above-discussed criteria, Habermas also points to the democratic deficit of the welfare state. Modern democracy is more about procuring mass loyalty than about real opportunities for citizens to influence laws and policies. Defining persons as clients of welfare state bureaucracies rather than as citizens expresses this problem. Persons are then defined as recipients of welfare services and not citizens engaged in formulating the needs underlying the welfare state (Habermas 1981, vol. 2: 506ff; see also Fraser 1990: Chaps. 7, 8). The understanding that problems of welfare state law primarily relate to the lack of democratic influence by citizens is more plausible than the analysis of law as steering media. Jütten (2011) suggests that this means to conceive of colonisation in terms of the normative expectations of citizens, namely, they should be able to take part in democratic law and policymaking.[11]

When Habermas outlines the condition of democratic legislation in *Between Facts and Norms*, it is largely in the background of the analysis of the democratic deficit of the welfare state, not the colonisation of the lifeworld. There are several merits to this approach, but there are also problems with how Habermas outlines the conditions for democratic participation, which I will discuss in the next chapter. Central to the present study is the dialectic of law. Habermas' analysis of colonisation acknowledges this dialectic. However, understanding it in terms of the distinction between lifeworld and system leads to several problems. A way out of this impasse is to pay attention to the kind of analysis that Menke advances of the modern legal form.

Normalisation and the Dialectic of Law

Similar to Habermas, Menke (2015: 286) argues that welfare state law (or social law) both enables and restricts freedom. Menke argues that welfare state law stresses taking part in social life. Social partaking is background for formulating social rights as the latter refers to key elements of social life, such as employment, family life, questions about health, and exposure to hazards and risks. Social rights are based on partaking, and the latter is simultaneously precondition for enjoying rights. In general, the materialisation of law and social rights in welfare states are emancipatory, enabling taking part in social life and equalising access to capacities and knowledge. Social rights tear down various kinds of privileges to education, healthcare, housing, and the like.

While emancipatory in certain respects, social partaking is also normalising. Menke is somewhat unclear about why this is the case. Sometimes he writes as if normalisation is inherent to any kind of sociality, meaning that there simply is no form of communication and participation without 'disciplining, forming and normalising' (Menke 2015: 286–my translation). That may of course be the case, but it does not allow us to distinguish normalisation from several other kinds of social domination. The way Menke relies on Foucault's (1976a, b, 1978) discussion about disciplinary and regulatory power suggests, however, more specific conceptions of normalisation.

In analysing these new forms of power, Foucault (1976b: 139ff, 1978) focused on the disciplining of individual bodies and the regulatory power over populations. Disciplinary power builds on establishing norms, in relation to which the examination of behaviour takes place and disciplining occurs. The latter is the attempt to bring behaviour into conformity with norms through different techniques. It is through these processes that the distinguishing of what is normal and abnormal takes place. Regulatory power or power connected to apparatuses of security is different in that it is about the plotting of 'different curves of normality, and the operation of normalization consists in establishing an interplay between these different distributions of normality and [in] acting to bring the most unfavorable in line with the more favorable' (Foucault 1978 [2007]: 63). In this case, the normal comes first and the norm is deduced on this basis, whereas the opposite holds true for discipline. Disciplinary and regulatory powers have important consequences for the character and functions of law. In normalising, society law comes to operate 'more and more as a norm' (Foucault 1976b: 144; see also Ewald 1990; Tadros 1998).

Normalisation in welfare states involves both discipline and regulatory power (Lemke 1997, Part 2: Chap. 3; Miller and Rose 2008). Discipline is more evident in institutions focused on shaping individual behaviour, and regulatory power is central for measures augmenting populations. Foucault (1975) analysed discipline by looking at the emergence and function of knowledge in institutions like prisons, suggesting that the same is the case with institutions like the army, schools, and so on. Among examples of regulatory power, the politics of health is an important example (Foucault 1976c; see also Rosen 1958). From the eighteenth century onwards, the focus of health is on improving the level of health for whole populations. Investigating the living environment or milieu became important and with this the knowledge of different factors that affect health. The development of social medicine in various forms became important for urban planning, housing, education, child rearing, and so on. It is sometimes said that 'social engineering' characterised the development of welfare states but more adequate would probably be to stress the role of doctors and metaphors like that of hygiene. Among the different technologies developed from the eighteenth century onwards, we find demographic estimates, calculations of life expectancy and levels of mortality, studies on the growth of population and the increase of wealth, factors affecting reproduction levels, etc.

Among the examples Habermas mentions, some involve disciplinary power. Therapeutic practices, focused on moulding individual behaviour, are perhaps the best example. In other cases, such as standard interpretations of needs, this involves both disciplinary and regulatory power, depending on how to understand 'standard'. Social assistance is an example. Decent living standards may seem to be about norms in the sense of laying down a certain minimum, providing the basis for calculating levels of social assistance. At the same time, decent living standard involves taking into account various types of factors that affect it. Moreover, what is decent living standard changes over time, depending on how most people live. Certainly, social assistance usually involves disciplinary power as well. Meeting with social workers, those assessing the situation of the person applying for social assistance, and so on, are examples (see Rauhut 2002; Marttila et al. 2010).

Moulding behaviour of children in schools in order to make them good pupils is an example of discipline, but the more this becomes dependent on knowing relevant factors affecting children's performance, such as dyslexia and other disabilities, the more it becomes regulatory. The reason is because then there is not only one norm but rather several normalities, it being central to understanding what is the normal learning process of children with dyslexia compared to other children, etc. In fact,

background. Habermas no longer pursues the theme of the dialectic of law. The reason is that he, in the meantime, abandons the colonisation analysis. Since he does that for good reasons, we cannot simply take up the perspective suggested in *The Theory of Communicative Action* again. There is a need to account for the dialectic of law in other ways. I have suggested that Menke's analysis of the modern form of rights and the legal form provide ways of doing so.

In this chapter, I pointed to how this involves reconsidering Habermas' analysis of law in *The Theory of Communicative Action* in two respects. First, in contrast to Habermas arguing that Hobbes' rendering of the lifeworld as formless misunderstands the rationalisation of the lifeworld, this characterisation follows from modern law involving relations between law and non-law. These relations imply that what is outside of law is formless, when viewed from the point of view of the form of law. Thus, Hobbes can be said to have captured key features of modern law. This interpretation differs from that of Habermas, who attributes Hobbes' understanding of the formlessness of the lifeworld to him developing law from a systems point of view. The point of this reconsideration is to allow for understanding the dialectic of law in ways that do not presuppose the system-lifeworld distinction. This does not mean that understanding society in these terms is without value, only that in case we want to address the dialectic of law, we need to do so in other ways than suggested by Habermas. This point applies to the second reconsideration as well, namely, how to view normalisation in welfare state law not as colonisation of the lifeworld but instead as outcome of disciplinary and regulatory power. This interpretation builds on familiar themes expressed by Foucault. Menke interprets this in terms of social partaking and private appropriation, thereby linking private law liberalism and the welfare state paradigm. Both dimensions to the reconsideration of Habermas' analysis are important for continuing an analysis of law that addresses how it is both condition for emancipation and domination.

Notes

1. An important dimension to the rationalisation of the lifeworld is the institutionalisation of discourses, for instance, in law-making processes through parliaments and more generally in public discussions. Habermas' (1962) analysis of the public sphere is important for what he later terms discourse. The principles he uncovers in the analysis of the literary

public, such as disregard of status and instead a focus on the equality and freedom of participants, the reciprocity of discussions, the openness regarding who can take part in discussions, and the difference between argument and person are important for what he later elaborates as discourse. There is an extensive scholarly discussion about communicative action and discourse (see Benhabib 1986: Chap. 8; McCarthy 1991; Rehg 1994). Discourses have to satisfy certain conditions if they are to count as reasonable discussions. Participants must have equal opportunities to make arguments, provide and contest reasons, and discuss the merits of reasons. Discourses must exclude all force except for the 'forceless force of the better argument' (Habermas 1981 [1984]: 24; see Allen 2012). Discourses also involve taking up perspectives of others and similar. For this reason, discourses are cooperative ventures for the searching of truth and normative rightness. In *Between Facts and Norms*, Habermas (1992: 369ff) discusses these conditions in relation to Joshua Cohen's (1989) formulation of criteria for deliberation (see also Chambers 1996; Rehg 1994).

2. Dissensus plays an important role in the politicisation of validity claims; critics sometimes overlook the importance of dissensus in Habermas' outlining of communicative action and discourse (see Markell 1997; Rostböll 2009; White and Farr 2012).
3. Habermas (1981, vol. 2: 208–228) discusses these dimensions of the lifeworld as its 'structural components': (a) culture, comprising the knowledge that supplies interpretations of the world, (b) society (or institutions) that defines group memberships and secures solidarity, and (c) personality, which relates to socialisation and identity formation, in particular, the competences required for taking part in communicative action. The differentiation of these components to the lifeworld makes up the modern characteristics of it and is thus an element of the rationalisation of the lifeworld. Baxter (2011: 173) argues that the idea of the structural components of the lifeworld does not contribute to our understanding of the lifeworld but may instead occlude it, especially since it is difficult to make use of this conception when discussing the legal anchoring of systems media (through private and public law). Baxter argues convincingly that the central ideas that Habermas wants to convey is possible to express in ways that are more direct.
4. Habermas later revises some of these ideas about the linguistification of the sacred, see Habermas (2012): 13ff.
5. Habermas follows Parsons' elaboration of the system media of money and administrative power, but unlike Parsons, Habermas does not view influence and value commitment as media (see also Chernilo 2002). Habermas uses the analogy between money and administrative power

suggested by Parsons but notes several differences between them. The major difference between these media is that whereas money does not need legitimation, power does. The reason for this is, first, because power can only be exercised through organisation—it is not a medium of circulation in the way that money is. Second, Habermas (1981 [1987], vol. 2: 271) argues that there are significant differences between the 'standard situations' of power and money. In his view, exchange relations do not disadvantage persons involved in calculating utility as such, whereas the exercise of power involves a structural disadvantage between persons giving orders and persons taking orders. This disadvantage, Habermas (1981 [1987], vol. 2: 271) argues, can be offset if those subjected to persons in power are 'in a position to contest [the claim] that the goals set are collectively desired or are, as we say, in the general interest. *It is only the reference to legitimizable collective goals that establishes the balance in the power relation built into the ideal-typical exchange relation from the start*'. The characterisation of exchange relations and power as order giving (and the contrast between them) involves several problems that I cannot address here, unfortunately. The scholarly discussions on these questions are extensive, see Honneth (1985): Chaps. 8–9; McCarthy (1985); Baxter (2011): Chaps. 1.3.

6. In fairness, we should also note that Habermas is more nuanced in *The Theory of Communicative Action* than critics argue. In addressing formally organised domains of action, such as state administration and business organisations, Habermas (1981 [1987]: 310f) argues that members of these organisations act communicatively 'only *with reservation*' because they 'know they *can* have recourse to formal regulations, not only in exceptional but in routine cases; there is no *necessity* for achieving consensus by communicative means'.
7. Related to this is the discussion on whether the conception of lifeworld is 'idyllic'. Baxter (2011: 176f, 2014) and Daniel Loick (2014) argue that Habermas' portrayal of the lifeworld has such connotations. Baxter argues that this is one reason for dropping the notion of the lifeworld altogether. While pointing to problems of Habermas' understanding of the lifeworld, I think the critique of the lifeworld connoting some 'idyll' is not very convincing (see also Wirts 2014).
8. Habermas (1981, vol. 2: 536ff) advances the interpretation that law as medium and law as institution correspond to different domains of law. Commercial and administrative law are examples of law as medium, and criminal law and constitutional law are examples of law as institution. This shows how Habermas, in discussing laws, tends to map analytical distinctions to specific domains. Therefore, it involves the same problems

as noted above with regard to system and social integration mapped onto institutions and spheres (see Deflem 2013: 81ff).

9. Formally organised are relations 'located in media-steered subsystems', Habermas (1981 [1987]: 309) argues, and these are first generated by positive law, for instance, as private law demarcates areas for private choice and public law the competences of legal officeholders. In these spheres, Habermas (1981 [1987]: 309) continues, 'legal norms replace the prelegal substratum of traditional morals'; therefore, law 'no longer starts from previously existing structures of communication'.
10. It is moreover difficult to see how it is possible to sustain the claim regarding which areas are regulated through law prior to the welfare state and which are not. As Habermas himself remarks, legal regulation of poor people and families existed prior to the welfare state. The interlinking of poverty and family on the one hand and system media on the other hand is also not new to the welfare state. Additionally, the welfare state is an advancement in several regards; for instance, concerning the treatment of women and men, adults and children, and more generally regarding the provision of social rights (see Loick 2014).
11. Jütten (2011) argues that Habermas' functionalist approach to colonisation is problematic, and he suggests supplementing it with a normative account of colonisation being wrong. Jütten (2011: 719) argues that 'there is no direct route from a social malfunction to a normative wrong' and suggests that we can understand the latter in terms of legitimate expectations on the part of participants: 'It is only when the social malfunction frustrates legitimate expectations that reification effects occur' (Jütten 2011: 719). The normative expectation of citizens is that they should have some substantial say in organising welfare state provisions and outlining laws and policies in the democratic state. When such opportunities are lacking and/or systematically biased against poor people, minorities, and so on, we face situations where the administrative-political system may appear as standing above and against citizens.

References

Allen, Amy. 2012. The Unforced Force of the Better Argument: Reason and Power in Habermas Political Theory. *Constellations* 19 (3): 353–368.

Apel, Karl-Otto. 1988. *Diskurs und Verantwortung. Das Problem des Übergangs zur postkonventionellen Moral.* Frankfurt: Suhrkamp.

Baxter, Hugh. 2011. *Habermas: The Discourse Theory of Law and Democracy.* Stanford: Stanford University Press.

Baxter, Hugh. 2014. Habermas' Sociological Theory of Law and Democracy: A Reply to Wirts, Flynn and Zurn. *Philosophy and Social Criticism* 40 (2): 225–234.

Benhabib, Seyla. 1986. *Critique, Norm, and Utopia. A Study of the Foundations of Critical Theory*. New York: Columbia University Press.

Blichner, Lars, and Anders Molander. 2008. Mapping Juridification. *European Law Journal* 14 (1): 36–54.

Chambers, Simone. 1996. *Reasonable Democracy. Jürgen Habermas and the Politics of Discourse*. Ithaca: Cornell University Press.

Chernilo, Daniel. 2002. The Theorization of Social Co-ordinations in Differentiated Societies: The Theory of Generalized Symbolic Media in Parsons, Luhmann and Habermas. *British Journal of Sociology* 53 (3): 431–449.

Cohen, Joshua. 1989. Deliberation and Democratic Legitimacy. In *The Good Polity. Normative Analysis of the State*, ed. Alan Hamlin and Philip Pettit, 17–34. Oxford: Blackwell.

Cook, Deborah. 2006. Staying Alive: Adorno and Habermas on Self-Preservation under Late Capitalism. *Rethinking Marxism* 18 (3): 433–447.

Cooke, Maeve. 1994. *Language and Reason. A Study of Habermas' Pragmatics*. Cambridge, MA: MIT Press.

Deflem, Mathieu. 2013. The Legal Theory of Jürgen Habermas: Between the Philosophy and the Sociology of Law. In *Law and Social Theory*, 2nd ed., ed. Reza Banakar and Max Travers, 75–90. Oxford: Hart.

Eder, Klaus. 1978. Zur Rationalisierungsproblematik des modernen Rechts. *Soziale Welt* 29 (2): 247–256.

Eder, Klaus. 1988. Critique of Habermas's Contribution to the Sociology of Law. *Law & Society Review* 22 (5): 931–944.

Ewald, Francois. 1990. Norms, Discipline, and the Law. *Representations* 30: 138–161.

Foucault, Michel. 1975 [1979]. *Discipline and Punish. The Birth of the Prison*, trans. Alan Sheridan. New York: Vintage.

Foucault, Michel. 1976a [2003]. *Society Must Be Defended. Lectures at the Collège de France, 1975–1976*, trans. David Macey. New York: Picador.

Foucault, Michel. 1976b [1980]. *History of Sexuality. Vol. 1: An Introduction*, trans. Robert Hurley. New York: Vintage.

Foucault, Michel. 1976c [1980]. The Politics of Health in the Eighteenth Century. In *Power/Knowledge: Selected Interviews and Other Writings 1972–1977*, ed. Colin Gordon, 166–182. New York: Pantheon Books.

Foucault, Michel. 1978 [2007]. *Security, Territory, Population. Lectures at the Collège de France, 1977–1978*, trans. Graham Burchell. Houndmills: Palgrave.

Fraser, Nancy. 1990. *Unruly Practices. Power, Discourse and Gender in Contemporary Social Theory*. Cambridge: Polity.

Habermas, Jürgen. 1962 [1990]. *Strukturwandel der Öffentlichkeit*. Frankfurt: Suhrkamp.

Habermas, Jürgen. 1973. *Legitimationsprobleme im Spätkapitalismus*. Frankfurt: Suhrkamp.

Habermas, Jürgen. 1981. *Theorie des kommunikativen Handelns*, 2 vols. Frankfurt: Suhrkamp. Translated by Thomas McCarthy as *The Theory of Communicative Action*, vol. 1 1984 and vol. 2 1987. Boston: Beacon Press.

Habermas, Jürgen. 1985. *Der philosophische Diskurs der Moderne*. Frankfurt: Suhrkamp.

Habermas, Jürgen. 1986. Entgegnung. In *Kommunikatives Handeln. Beiträge zu Jürgen Habermas' Theorie des kommunikativen Handelns*, ed. Axel Honneth and Hans Joas, 327–405. Frankfurt: Suhrkamp.

Habermas, Jürgen. 1991. *Erläuterungen zur Diskursethik*. Frankfurt: Suhrkamp.

Habermas, Jürgen. 1992. *Faktizität und Geltung. Beiträge zur Diskurstheorie des Rechts und des demokratischen Rechtsstaats*. Frankfurt: Suhrkamp. Translated by William Rehg as *Between Facts and Norms. Contributions to a Discourse Theory of Law and Democracy*. Cambridge: Polity Press, 1996.

Habermas, Jürgen. 2012. *Nachmetaphysisches Denken II. Aufsätze und Repliken*. Berlin: Suhrkamp.

Honneth, Axel. 1985. *Kritik der Macht. Reflexionsstufen einer kritischen Gesellschaftstheorie*. Frankfurt: Suhrkamp.

Horkheimer, Max, and Theodor W. Adorno. 1944/1947. *Dialektik der Aufklärung*. Frankfurt: Fischer, 2006. Translated by John Cumming as *Dialectic of Enlightenment*. London: Verso, 1997.

Jütten, Timo. 2011. The Colonization Thesis: Habermas on Reification. *International Journal of Philosophical Studies* 19 (5): 701–727.

Jütten, Timo. 2013. Habermas and Markets. *Constellations* 20 (4): 587–603.

Kohlberg, Lawrence. 1981. *Essays on Moral Development, vol. 1: The Philosophy of Moral Development*. San Francisco: Harper & Row.

Kübler, Friedrich (ed.). 1985. *Verrechtlichung von Wirtschaft, Arbeit und sozialer Solidarität: vergleichende Analysen*. Baden-Baden: Nomos.

Lemke, Thomas. 1997. *Eine Kritik der politischen Vernunft Foucaults Analyse der modernen Gouvernementalität*. Hamburg: Argument Verlag.

Loick, Daniel. 2014. Juridification and Politics: From the Dilemma of Juridification to the Paradoxes of Rights. *Philosophy and Social Criticism* 40 (8): 757–778.

Lukács, Georg. 1923 [1968]. *Geschichte und Klassenbewusstsein*. Darmstadt: Hermann Luchterhand Verlag.

Markell, Patchen. 1997. Contesting Consensus: Rereading Habermas on the Public Sphere. *Constellations* 3 (3): 377–400.

Marttila, Anneli, Margaret Whitehead, Krysia Canvin, and Bo Burström. 2010. Controlled and Dependent: Experiences of Living on Social Assistance in Sweden. *International Journal of Social Welfare* 19 (2): 142–151.

McCarthy, Thomas. 1985 [1991]. Complexity and Democracy: The Seducements of Systems Theory. In *Ideals and Illusions. On Reconstruction and Deconstruction in Contemporary Critical Theory*, ed. T. McCarthy, 152–180. Cambridge, MA: MIT Press.

McCarthy, Thomas. 1991. Practical Discourse: On the Relation of Morality to Politics. In *Ideals and Illusions. On Reconstruction and Deconstruction in Contemporary Critical Theory*, ed. T. McCarthy, 181–199. Cambridge, MA: MIT Press.

Menke, Christoph. 2015. *Kritik der Rechte*. Berlin: Suhrkamp.

Miller, Peter, and Nikolas Rose. 2008. *Governing the Present*. Cambridge: Polity.

Niesen, Peter, and Oliver Eberl. 2009. Demokratischer Positivismus: Habermas und Maus. In *Neue Theorien des Rechts*, ed. Sonja Buckel, Ralph Christensen, and Andreas Fischer-Lescano, 3–26. Stuttgart: Lucius & Lucius.

Outhwaite, William. 2009. *Habermas—A Critical Introduction*, 2nd ed. Cambridge: Polity.

Peters, Bernhard. 1994. On Reconstructive Legal and Political Theory. *Philosophy & Social Criticism* 20 (4): 101–134.

Rauhut, Daniel. 2002. *Fattigvård, socialbidrag och synen på fattigdom i Sverige 1918–1997*. Stockholm: Almqvist & Wiksell.

Rehg, William. 1994. *Insight and Solidarity. The Discourse Ethics of Jürgen Habermas*. Berkeley: University of California Press.

Rose, Nikolas, and Mariana Valverde. 1998. Governed by Law? *Social Legal Studies* 7 (4): 541–551.

Rosen, George. 1958 [2015]. *A History of Public Health* (revised and expanded edition). Baltimore: Johns Hopkins University Press.

Rostböll, Christian. 2009. Dissent, Criticism, and Transformative Political Action in Deliberative Democracy. *Critical Review of International Social and Political Philosophy* 12 (1): 19–36.

Scheuerman, William. 2013. Capitalism, Law, and Social Criticism. *Constellations* 20 (4): 571–686.

Sohn-Rethel, Alfred. 1972. *Geistige und körperliche Arbeit: zur Theorie der gesellschaftlichen Synthesis*. Suhrkamp: Frankfurt.

Tadros, Victor. 1998. Between Governance and Discipline: The Law and Michel Foucault. *Oxford Journal of Legal Studies* 18 (1): 75–103.

Teubner, Gunther (ed.). 1988. *Dilemmas of Law in the Welfare State*. New York: Walter de Gruyter.

White, Stephen, and Evan Robert Farr. 2012. "No-Saying" in Habermas. *Political Theory* 40 (1): 32–57.

Wirts, Amelia. 2014. A Defence of the Lifeworld: The Source of Normativity in a Democracy. *Philosophy and Social Criticism* 40 (2): 214–223.

CHAPTER 4

The Reconstruction of the System of Rights

Abstract This chapter addresses Habermas' reconstruction of private and public autonomy. Habermas points to an important problem in how modern legal paradigms, both liberal and welfare state law, rely on private autonomy. This shows the importance of reconstructing the internal relation between private and public autonomy, bringing out the political autonomy of citizens. Habermas suggests that his elaboration of the system of rights shows the co-originality of private and public autonomy. While this project is important, it is also doubtful that modern law is adequate for showing this co-originality. The reason is that modern law largely relies on private autonomy, reflected in the modern concept of rights.

Keywords Habermas · Democracy · System of rights · Autonomy · Law

Introduction

The central question in *Between Facts and Norms* is how citizens may influence and program system media by legislation, thus, using law as a language for the realisation of their autonomy. In relation to the shaping of modern societies through the systems of money and administrative power, Habermas (1992 [1996]: 41) argues that system media remain under pressure of legitimation:

M. Spång, *Emancipation, Democracy and the Modern Critique of Law*, International Political Theory, DOI 10.1007/978-3-319-62890-5_4

> Even the systemic integration achieved through money and power *ought*, in accordance with the constitutional self-understanding of the legal community, to remain dependent on the socially integrative process of civic self-determination.

Elaborating on this 'ought' in ways that are adequate for functionally differentiated societies is central for the undertaking in *Between Facts and Norms*. Habermas does so through reconstructing the relation between private and public autonomy, attempting to show how they are co-original and mutually supporting each other. The core of the reconstruction is the system of rights, rights that citizens need to recognise with each other when they want to regulate their life together through positive law. Reconstructing the relation between private and public autonomy is necessary for overcoming the problem of how both liberal and welfare state law involve an emphasis on private autonomy.

The dialectic of law, important to the analysis in *The Theory of Communicative Action*, does not play any significant role in *Between Facts and Norms*. Instead of discussing welfare state law as inherently dilemmatic, Habermas suggests that the problematic feature of this kind of law, in both enabling and restricting autonomy, is possible to explain through the dialectic of legal and factual equality. As discussed in the first chapters, Habermas argues that problematic features of welfare state law stem from the unresolved tension between private and public autonomy. I tried to show how focusing on the dialectic of law is different from this and argued for the relevance of addressing this dialectic. In the previous chapter, I attempted to show how it is possible to address the dialectic of law in ways that do not depend on Habermas' colonisation analysis. It is against this background that I focus in this chapter on Habermas' analysis in *Between Facts and Norms*.

Reconstructing the Relation Between Private and Public Autonomy

The central focus in *Between Facts and Norms* is on how to elaborate the conditions for the possibility of self-legislation by citizens in functionally differentiated societies. This involves reconstructing the system of rights enabling democratic law making, that is, the generation of legitimate law. The system of rights consists of the basic categories of rights citizens have to recognise each other when they want to regulate their life together through positive law. Before coming to specify these rights, there are of course several preparatory steps to take, among them to answer questions as to why citizens should want to make use of positive law in regulating their life together.

Habermas does not think that we are under any moral obligation to use positive law for regulating our lives together. There are, however, functional reasons for why law is an appropriate medium, Habermas thinks. The role of law in constituting and organising the modern state and the modern capitalist economy is an example, as is also the rationalisation of the lifeworld. While the latter opens up for freedom in several respects, it also means assigning communicative action a burden for social integration that it cannot bear. Law relieves communicative action of some of its integrative burden and resolves the problem of 'how the validity and acceptance of a social order can be stabilized once communicative actions [has] become autonomous' (Habermas 1992 [1996]: 25). Unlike the spellbinding authority of the sacred in archaic societies, which fused together facticity and validity, the bonding or binding character of modern law is built around the tensions between the facticity and the validity of law. Law does not simply perform stabilising functions but does so in ways that conform to the rationalisation of the lifeworld. Law enables 'unfettered communication to unburden itself of socially integrative achievements without compromising itself', Habermas (1992 [1996]: 37) argues.

In discussing the tensions of validity and facticity of law, we should note that Habermas addresses both the external and internal tensions between the validity and the facticity of law. The external dimension concerns the relation between the validity of law and societal facticity, for instance, how law often enough, in Habermas' (1992: 59f) words, only confers the semblance of legitimacy on social power. The role played by corporations, interest organisations, lobbying groups, and the like in policy and lawmaking are examples of this as are also the power of bureaucracies with regard to political decision-making. While important to the empirical analyses of actual policy and lawmaking processes, I will not say so much about it here (see Deflem 1994, 2008: Chaps. 7–10; Staats 2004). Instead, I focus on the internal relation between the facticity and validity of law, which Habermas also spends most time in discussing. The facticity dimension internal to the legal medium refers in particular to the enforceability of laws but also to the fact that rights enable individuals to pursue their own interests. The validity dimension refers to the processes through which enacting of legitimate law takes place, that is, the democratic law making process.

The fact that rights enable persons to pursue their own interests makes the distinction between private and public law relevant. Private law plays a central role in the emergence of modern legal orders, enabling persons to engage in strategic action. Law anchors strategic action in the lifeworld through private autonomy, especially regarding property and individual contract. The elaboration of rights in the social contract tradition reflects this. Habermas incorporates this understanding of rights in his reconstruction, first by noting that persons may obey laws because they make up outer restrictions to strategic action and second by noting that all rights, including political rights, are 'subjective rights'. The latter entails that citizens have the option to take part in political action or refrain from doing so. Yet, since the legal medium is supposed to stabilise interaction not only factually but also legitimately, it is central to stress the intrinsic relation between positive law and democratic lawmaking. For this reason, it is important to view the ability to pursue interests and engage in strategic action in the context of public law and democratic lawmaking. As discussed in the previous chapter, Habermas shares Durkheim's understanding that private law is not free standing and does not constitute a stable order by itself. What is required, Habermas argues, are norms that on the one hand open up for strategic action and yet link this to social integration based on communicative action. A way out of this problem, Habermas (1992 [1996]: 26f) claims, is that actors '*come to some understanding* about the *normative regulation of strategic interactions*'.

The key in this regard is that legal norms both constitute outer restrictions to strategic action and have a socially integrating force by imposing obligations. Legitimately, imposing obligations are possible only through democratic processes of lawmaking. This calls for a fundamental shift regarding the internal relation between facticity and validity of law. Whereas the facticity of law with regard to enforcement of it refers to norm compliance, the facticity of lawmaking differs from this (Habermas 1992: 50ff). It means that the positivity of law, that is, how it is enacted in political processes, comes into focus. The permission to make laws that impose obligations on individuals stems from the democratic process in which every citizen can take part:

> The positivity of law is bound up with the promise that democratic processes of lawmaking justify the presumption that enacted norms are rationally acceptable. Rather than displaying the facticity of an arbitrary, absolutely contingent choice, the positivity of law expresses the legitimate will that stems from a presumptively rational self-legislation of politically autonomous citizens. (Habermas 1992 [1996]: 33)

The genesis of legitimate law, thus, comes into focus by the shift from norm compliance to legislation. Legitimacy cannot refer to legality as such; recall Habermas faulting Weber for holding the view that legality suffices for legitimacy. Neither can the securing of private rights provide the basis for the legitimacy of law. Habermas agrees with Durkheim that contracts refer to the legality of the legal-political order and this in turn to the legitimacy of this order, that is, to the constitutional principles of human rights and popular sovereignty. Nor is the legitimacy of positive law secured through subsuming it to natural law. The older natural law theories from late antiquity to the Middle Ages built on assumptions about human nature, the order of the cosmos, or God, all of which are assumptions that we cannot sustain under post-metaphysical conditions (Habermas 1985: Chap. 12, 1992: Chaps. 1 and 2). Moreover, Habermas thinks that it is not possible to subsume modern law to morality, thereby expressing his difference with several other political and legal theorists working in the Kantian tradition. There is no other way than to address the legitimacy of laws through democratic lawmaking, Habermas contends, which explains what he has in mind when saying that '[t]he process of legislation thus represents the place in the legal system where social integration first occurs' (Habermas 1992 [1996]: 32).

The Principle of Democracy and the Legal Form

The possibility of challenging validity claims is a central feature of communicative action. When discussing validity claims, we participate in an argumentative practice that Habermas calls discourse. In the 1980s, Habermas developed his conception of discourse for reformulating Kantian ethics (see Habermas 1983, 1991). In *Between Facts and Norms*, Habermas uses the idea of discourse but adapts the principle of discourse so that it covers both moral and legal norms. It is not possible to apply the discourse ethical principle to democracy straight off because that would amount to subsuming democracy to morality (Habermas 1992:

Sect. 3.2; compare Touri 1989). Moral reasons do play important roles in democratic lawmaking processes, but participants may use other reasons as well. Both pragmatic reasons about what is the most efficient way to achieve specific objectives and also ethical reasons, which refer to the common life of citizens as members of a specific political community play a role. Moreover, fair compromises concerning interests are also important in democratic processes of lawmaking (Habermas 1992: 133ff).

For these reasons, the principle of discourse that Habermas elaborates on in *Between Facts and Norms* is more abstract than in his earlier account. The general discourse principle applies to all norms, both moral and legal norms. It is then possible to distinguish between two principles, the moral principle and the democratic principle, respectively, based on the general principle of discourse. The reason for this being possible is that the dissolution of ethical life and the rationalisation of the lifeworld have led to the differentiation of law and morality. The principle of democracy specifies the general discourse principle with regard to norms that appear in legal form. The principle of democracy refers to legitimate lawmaking and runs as follows: '[O]nly those statutes may claim legitimacy that can meet with the assent (*Zustimmung*) of all citizens in a discursive process of legislation that in turn has been legally constituted' (Habermas 1992 [1996]: 110).[1] This principle, Habermas continues, 'explains the performative meaning of the practice of self-determination on the part of legal consociates who recognize one another as free and equal members of an association they have joined voluntarily' (1992 [1996]: 110). The democratic community is a legal community, and the principle of democracy applies to legal norms. The principle of democracy comes about through the application of the principle of discourse to the legal form. Habermas' understanding of the legal form involves the three kinds of abstraction discussed in the first chapter.

The Generation of the Principle of Democracy

The legal form is required for outlining the principle of democracy in Habermas' view. This goes not only for the definition of the principle, as a matter of citizens debating the merits of laws, but also for the generation of the democracy principle. In this regard, a contradiction arises in Habermas' reconstruction. This inconsistency concerns the question of the legal prefiguring of democracy.

The principle of democracy comes about by applying the principle of discourse to the legal form. Habermas (1992 [1996]: 121) formulates this in the following way: '[T]he principle of democracy derives from the interpenetration of the discourse principle and the legal form'. A few lines later on, we find a slightly different formulation. Habermas (1992 [1996]: 122) states that 'the legal code, or legal form, and the mechanism for producing legitimate law—hence the democratic principle—is *co-originally* constituted'. These statements seem to pull in different directions. Stressing that the principle of democracy is generated by the application of the principle of discourse to the legal form requires that the legal form has to be in place for democracy to be possible. It is not possible to conceive of democracy outside of the (modern) legal form. The other formulation gestures to a more radical claim, that is, the legal form and the principle of democracy come about at the same time.

How to interpret Habermas at this point is, however, not easy. It is difficult because it is not entirely clear to discern if Habermas sees any difference between legal form and legal code (see also Baxter 2011: 69). Some statements suggest that there are no differences between them; the co-original constituting of the legal code or the legal form and the principle of democracy suggest that legal code and legal form are the same. However, other statements suggest otherwise. When Habermas says that the principle of democracy is generated through applying the principle of discourse to the legal form, the latter is different from the legal code. The legal code refers to subjective rights. Ingeborg Maus (1996: 842) highlights this difference when she says that the 'application of the discourse principle to the legal form gives rise "equiprimordially" (on either side of the circular process) on the one hand to the principle of democracy and on the other to subjective private rights which are identical to the legal code'. According to this interpretation, the legal code refers to subjective private rights regarding *inter alia* liberties, membership in the legal community, and legal protection. This is different from the legal form, which refers to the forms of abstraction discussed in the second chapter.

Following Maus' interpretation, the two ways in which Habermas formulates the relation between legal form and the principle of democracy does not pull in different directions but rather affirm each other. The legal form is presupposition for modern democracy, and it is not possible to make sense of democracy in any other way. This interpretation is in line with Habermas' overall argument about the legal medium.

However, there are additional remarks made by Habermas that suggest that there is perhaps something to the more radical interpretation. This is evident when Habermas (1992 [1996]: 111) says that the principle of democracy has the function to *'steer the production of the legal medium itself'*.

Democracy steering the production of the legal medium may only mean enacting laws through democratic processes. However, Habermas seems to have something more radical in mind by stressing that democracy should steer the production of the legal medium. Even though the legal form is presupposition for democracy, it cannot remain simply a presupposition. At the very least, democracy steering the legal medium must refer to citizens making the language of law their own language. While Habermas (1992: 160f) says that citizens cannot choose the language through which they are to realise their autonomy, the language cannot remain simply a given. Making law their own language may mean that citizens get socialised into using this language, but socialisation is a weak interpretation of democracy steering the production of the legal medium. We may interpret the argument in a stronger way, suggesting that citizens hold some constitutive power with regard to the language of realising their autonomy. Most of what Habermas has to say about democracy in modern functionally differentiated societies would suggest that he does not hold this strong view.

It is, therefore, unclear what democracy steering the production of the legal medium means, more specifically. To interpret this as meaning, the constituting of the legal medium is too strong. To interpret it as the socialising dimension of law is too weak. A third possibility is to interpret it as meaning the possibility of asking whether law is an appropriate medium for the realisation of autonomy. In principle, Habermas acknowledges this possibility since we are under no obligation to make use of the language of law. However, because no one has been able to point to an alternative language, this questioning remains somewhat empty and abstract for Habermas. Yet, in my view, this third understanding seems to be a plausible interpretation. While it may seem difficult to imagine what the problematisation of law as collective practice involves, something close to it is what we find in several social movements over the past 150 years, from the labour movements and the criticism of juridical socialism to contemporary social movements. Recurrent questions in social movements have involved the problematisation of law and rights, and the possibilities and limitations of this vocabulary.

The System of Rights

The system of rights outlined in the third chapter of *Between Facts and Norms* is the centrepiece of Habermas' reconstruction. This system outlines those rights 'citizens must accord one another if they want to legitimately regulate their common life by means of positive law' (Habermas 1992 [1996]: 82). The system of rights is supposed to give equal weight to citizens' private and public autonomy. Central to the modern legal form is the idea of rights. The legal medium presupposes rights that define the legal subject as bearer of rights. Habermas assumes that rights, in line with the modern natural law tradition, refer to the private autonomy of persons; rights specify liberties. The right to liberties contained in modern law is not simply 'the right to liberties in general but the right of each person to equal liberties', Habermas (1992 [1996]: 120) argues and in this he follows the tradition from Kant to Rawls.

Similar to social contract theories, Habermas (1992 [1996]: 118) argues that rights 'should be introduced first of all from the perspective of a nonparticipant'. However, the theorist cannot specify in detail what these rights entail; that is ultimately the job of citizens, who act as authors of laws, including constitutional laws. When introduced from the perspective of the non-participating theorist, therefore, rights refer to basic categories of rights. The first three categories of rights, Habermas (1992 [1996]: 122) argues, generate 'the legal code itself by defining the status of legal persons': (1) 'Basic rights that result from the politically autonomous elaboration of the *right to the greatest possible measure of equal individual liberties*'. These rights require in turn (2) rights that concern 'the *status of a member* in a voluntary association of consociates under law' and (3) rights that relate to the possibility of claiming rights, what Habermas calls the 'actionability' of rights, and the legal protection of individuals. Habermas (1992 [1996]: 122) argues that the legal code defines the status of legal persons equipped with rights and comes about, 'simply from the application of the discourse principle to the medium of law as such'. Even though these three categories of rights express ideas familiar from the history of rights articulated in relation to the state, Habermas argues that we should not understand the categories of basic rights in this way. We are at this stage in the reconstruction not assuming that there is a state. The rights 'only regulate the relationships among freely associated citizens *prior to* any legally organized state authority' (Habermas 1992 [1996]: 122). This is consonant with Habermas'

Kantian understanding of the social contract; the contract is not about constituting the state but about outlining an idea of legal sociation (*Vergesellschaftung*).[2]

The next step involves introducing the kind of rights that make it possible for citizens to become authors of law: (4) 'Basic rights to equal opportunities to participate in processes of opinion- and will-formation in which citizens exercise their *political autonomy* and through which they generate legitimate law' (Habermas 1992 [1996]: 123). Similar to most other theorists of democracy, Habermas thinks that equal opportunities to take part in politics require that social rights be granted to citizens (see Bohman 2000: Chap. 3; Dahl 1989: Chap. 8, 2007). Opportunities to take part in politics must be real and not merely formal opportunities. Habermas, therefore, endorses the argument made by Rawls (1993: lecture 8.7) regarding the fair value of political liberties. Thus, in order for citizens to be able to utilise the other rights, they have to enjoy (5) basic rights 'to the provision of living conditions that are socially, technologically, and ecologically safeguarded' (Habermas 1992 [1996]: 123; see also Olson 1998).

Political rights hold a central position in the system of rights because it is through making use of them that citizens work out the content of the basic rights. This is the reason for Habermas' formulation of basic rights as the 'result from the politically autonomous elaboration'. This plays an important role in the argument that private and public autonomy is co-original. The first three categories, which are central expressions of the legal subject and its private autonomy (liberty), are necessary for establishing the legal code as such. Private autonomy is a cornerstone of modern law and a presupposition for public autonomy. Public autonomy is at the same time a presupposition for private autonomy because the specific shaping of rights must be the outcome of political processes of self-legislation by citizens. Modern law is not simply the stabilisation of interaction between private legal subjects, but it presupposes legitimate procedures of lawmaking. The latter is only possible if the citizens as addresses of law are also able to become authors of law. We, thus, have to keep in mind two things, Habermas (1992 [1996]: 126) claims: first that 'the first three categories of rights are unsaturated placeholders', which have to be specified through constitution making and ordinary legislation but also, second, that they guide these legislating practices. The first three categories of rights give, as Habermas (1992

[1996]: 126) expresses it, 'teeth to what Hobbes and Rousseau found so important: the rationalizing character of the legal form as such'.

Habermas' claim to have shown how private and public autonomy is co-original and mutually supporting has been much discussed. In the early reception of the work, some critics argued that Habermas privileges private autonomy by introducing the rights relating to private autonomy first and arguing that these rights are inherent in the legal form as such (Kupka 1994). Since political autonomy is possible only through the system of rights, it seems that rights relating to private autonomy come prior to rights relating to public autonomy. Other critics argued in contrast that Habermas stresses public autonomy too much and that his reconstruction amounts to the subordination of liberties to public autonomy (Larmore 1993). Other scholars argued that these interpretations reflect a misunderstanding of Habermas' elaboration on the co-originality of private and public autonomy (Günther 1994). More specifically, what is often misunderstood is the nature of the circle between private and public autonomy and the role of the theorist in relation to citizens' political action. Maus (1996: 839) directs attention to the latter, stressing that there is a difference between how the theorist presents the categories of rights and how citizens make use of them. The fact that Habermas specifies the basic rights in terms of their politically autonomous elaboration means that whereas citizens cannot engage in democratic lawmaking without assuming the legal code, established through the basic rights 1–3, the latter rights are not presuppositions for political autonomy. Maus argues that central in this regard is the change of perspective involved in Habermas' presentation. Habermas states that one should begin with the rights from a social contract point of view outside of political practices, telling 'citizens which rights they *should* acknowledge mutually if they are to legitimately regulate their living together by means of positive law' (Habermas 1992 [1996]: 126).

In stipulating the political rights, which enable citizens to work out the specific content and shape of the basic rights, Habermas changes perspective. This change is required in order for the theorist not becoming an expert that tells the citizens how they are going to specify the rights established through the legal code. 'As a *democratic* theorist', Maus (1996: 839) notes, Habermas has to renounce the social contract perspective 'in favor of the political autonomy of constitutional lawmaking and law-giving citizens who first develop these rights from their own vantage point'. The theorist cannot tell citizens what the more specific content of their political autonomous working out should be but only specify the conditions that enable them to act in a politically autonomous manner. These enabling conditions build on reconstructing historical practices of constitution making and legislative processes. As Maus (1996: 839) makes clear, 'Habermas ultimately understands his system of rights as a generalizing reconstruction of the self-understanding on which historically known democratic constitutions and declarations of rights are necessarily based'.

The Constitutional-Democratic State

The reconstruction of the system of rights, Habermas argues, outlines the kind of sociation that takes place through the form of law, the combining of private and public autonomy, without this presupposing the state. Besides the question about whether or not this involves a private law construct, it also raises questions about the relationship between the modern state form and the modern legal form. In *Between Facts and Norms*, Habermas (1992 [1996]: 132) argues that we have to bring state power into the picture if we want to understand how the system of rights is 'put to work'. It turns out (we may add, fortunately for Habermas) that the relationship between law and political power is reciprocal. Rights take on effect, Habermas (1992 [1996]: 133) argues, 'only by organizations that make collectively binding decisions' and conversely 'these decisions owe their collective bindingness to the legal form in which they are clad'. Moreover, this relationship between political power and law is understandable as an evolutionary process whereby binding law and political power constitute themselves co-originally.

Habermas provides a highly stylised account of the evolution from traditional to modern societies to back up this claim, an account that is at odds with much of what we know about modern state formation processes, highlighted by historical sociologists such as Charles Tilly (1975, 1992) and others (see Giddens 1985). Habermas pays little attention to the violence involved in modern state formation processes and therefore risks disregarding traces of violence when discussing the intertwining of political power and law. This is not just a general problem because Habermas' analysis of the evolution of law and political power has a more specific aim, namely to tie the administrative and communicative power together. The reason for tying together political power and law in the stylised account of the transition from archaic to modern societies is very much that this provides the backdrop for arguing that administrative and communicative power are combined in processes of legislation. This, in turn, is important for Habermas' argument that positive law and democratic lawmaking goes hand in hand. The question of violence and law is widely discussed. Benjamin (1921) famously argued that it is not possible to discard the violence that is element of lawmaking. Several theorists in the tradition of the modern critique of law have argued similar to Menke (2010) that law putting an end to violence (revenge) presupposes that persons subsume themselves to law, judge themselves in the light of law and understand themselves as legal beings. This is the 'curse of law', Menke (2010: 9) argues, because subsuming to law does not tie in with any release from 'its identifying power'. Law holds the individual captive; it implies a form of violence that consists of individuals judging themselves in ways that do not involve release but is instead curse. This kind of violence is internal to law, related to how law works, 'the violence of losing one's subjectivity precisely by enacting it' (Menke 2010: 9). Habermas pays little attention to the problems of law and violence. Pointing to it does not mean to deny the civilisational role of law in ending violence, more specifically putting an end to the justice of revenge, but to keeping in mind that accounting for the intertwining of law and political power without attending to traces of violence in law is one-sided.

The Democratic Circulation of Power

The reconstruction of the system of rights is supposed to bring out how citizens are authors of law. Habermas (1992 [1996]: 187) argues that central to the idea of political authorship is that '[p]olitically autonomous citizens can understand themselves as authors of the law to which they submit as private subjects only if legitimately generated law also determines the *direction* in which political power circulates'. The democratic circulation of power is central to the discourse theoretical reading of popular sovereignty. By popular sovereignty, Habermas (1992 [1996]: 170) understands the idea that 'all political power derives from the communicative power of citizens'. Habermas wants to avoid a too concrete understanding of people; therefore, he interprets popular sovereignty in communication terms.[3]

The democratic circulation of political power builds on understanding political power as communicative power on the one hand and as administrative power on the other hand. In order to explicate what communicative power means, Habermas enlists Arendt (1958: part 5) and her reflections on power arising when people come together to speak and act. Habermas pays little attention to the theorising of political action that Arendt engaged in and makes use of her analysis primarily for conceptualising the kind of power generated by citizens in public spheres and through civil society organisations.[4] Habermas is interested in how communicative power, generated by citizens coming together to speak and to act, is related to lawmaking, contending that '[l]aw joins forces *from the outset* with a communicative power that engenders legitimate law' (Habermas 1992 [1996]: 149; see also Günther 1998; Preuss 1998).

Central in this regard is the question of how communicative power transforms into administrative power when it passes through legislative processes. Following Bernhard Peters (1993: Sect. 9.1), Habermas discusses this in terms of 'sluices' of the political system, in particular the legislature, whereby communicative power enters the political system and becomes the basis of legislation.[5] Citizens generate communicative power in the periphery, in public spheres and civil society organisations, from which it enters the centre of the political system, such as parliament, government, and courts. When processed in legislatures and other institutional complexes of the state, communicative power transforms into administrative power. This describes the official circulation of power in a democracy (Habermas 1992: 435ff; see also Baxter 2011: Sects. 2.4 and 4.3.1; Peters 1993: 340ff).

Actual decision-making in the political system often deviates from this circulation of power (Habermas 1992: 431ff). In the routine mode of the political system, the government and the administration prepare the bulk of legislation and policies. Powerful actors, such as corporations and various types of interest organisations, are able to exert much influence on laws and policies. Different professions and expert networks likewise play important roles in policymaking processes. Most citizens play only marginal roles in these processes, with their political participation often being restricted to elections and referendums. Even during election campaigns, most citizens are more an audience listening to political debates and watching the political game than active participants (see Manin 1997: Chap. 6). In addition, several bodies and agencies responsible for, among others, service provision, economic and monetary policies, and risk assessment and so on are independent from the legislature and the government to varying degrees (Loughlin 2010: 448ff).

Habermas does not think that the routine mode is a problem as such. Habermas' ideas have little in common with models of participatory democracy, which stresses the extensive participation of citizens in more day-to-day politics (see Bachrach and Botwinick 1992; Fung and Olin Wright 2003). What matters for Habermas are the possibilities of citizens to interrupt the routine mode and assert the democratic circulation of power. This is likely in times of crisis, when an 'activated periphery' can play the decisive role (Habermas 1992 [1996]: 358; see also Cordero 2014; Peters 1993: 346ff).[6] Interrupting the routine mode requires that public spheres and civil society actors are adequate 'sensory systems' for detecting and articulating inequalities, injustices and so on. Moreover, civil society actors and social movements must be able to amplify what citizens articulate in public debates and influence parliaments and other decision-making bodies. It is not self-evident that public spheres and civil society in a given political system have these capacities. Habermas (2011) points, for instance, to problems in this regard when discussing European public spheres and politics within the EU.

Communicative power thus plays a central role in Habermas' account of the democratic circulation of power. However, it is also an ambivalent notion because it has two interrelated but distinct meanings. When Habermas discusses communicative power in relation to Arendt, it relates to the kind of power that emerges from citizens' more or less spontaneous political action (Arendt 1958: part V, 1969). When addressing the link between communicative and administrative power, it is instead central, in Habermas' (1992 [1996]: 371) view, that 'public influence is transformed into communicative power only after it passes through the filters of the institutionalized *procedures* of democratic opinion- and will-formation and enters through parliamentary debates into legitimate lawmaking'. Habermas thinks that this understanding of communicative power is in line with Arendt's conception but this is far from evident, in particular since Habermas (1992: 449f) argues that a central function of legislatures is to filter opinions, to synthesise views and render them more reasonable. Historically, this is not the radical view of parliaments but the view taken by those who have feared that the opinions of ordinary citizens are too unreasonable and unruly. Those fearing that ordinary citizens would make claims about using political power in ways that posed threats to the economic order, and so on, have stressed the importance of filtering opinions. These discussions also influence contemporary understandings. Habermas (1973) previously focused on the problems involved in the filtering of opinions. Instead of rendering opinions reasonable, Habermas and other scholars directed attention towards how filtering weeded out what is radical and controversial (see Demirovic 1997: Offe 1989).

The focus on legislation illustrates a certain legal prefiguring of politics. Besides the discussion on communicative power, another example is how Habermas pays little attention to the fact that changing laws is only one of the focuses in social movements. Pressing for legislative changes and making claims in the legal system are certainly important strategies, but there are several other types of action as well. In fact, social movements have focused as much, if not more, on changing societal relations through other strategies than legislation, involving negotiations with societal actors, influencing common sense through opinion work and consciousness raising as well as establishing alternative orders, such as collectives, cooperatives and alternative education institutions (see Giugni, McAdam and Tilly 1999; Tarrow 1998; Tilly 2013). The relative neglect of these forms of politics is somewhat surprising, especially since the account of communicative action allows for connecting everyday politicisation and mobilisation in social movements. The reason Habermas pays little attention to these features of public spheres and social movements stems, to no small degree, from the legal focus adopted in his work. This is one of the reasons behind Honneth's (2011: 613ff) argument that the focus on law in much of the contemporary discussions about freedom and justice goes astray.

Honneth (2011 [2014]: 329) argues that the focus on law is understandable because it is part of the modern self-understanding that laws and policies formulated in democratic political processes make up the 'active centre of the entire institutional order'. At the same time, this view is misleading because it overemphasises the role that law plays in integrating modern societies. It neglects the complex patterns of realising freedom in different social spheres, in personal relationships, on labour and consumer markets, and so on, as argued by Honneth. Moreover, the focus on law does not sufficiently take into account how social and political struggles are central for societal transformations:

> The motor and the medium of the historical process of realizing institutionalized principles of freedom is not the law, at least not in the first

> instance, but social struggles over the appropriate understanding of these principles and the resulting changes of behaviour. Therefore, the fact that contemporary theories of justice are guided almost exclusively by the legal paradigm is a theoretical folly. (Honneth 2011 [2014]: 329)

Paradigms of Law and Private Autonomy

As already discussed, Habermas argues that both the liberal and the welfare state legal paradigms involve an emphasis on private autonomy. As a consequence, both lose sight of how central political autonomy is for legitimate lawmaking. In order to continue the welfare state project on a higher level of reflection, Habermas argues that we have to understand the co-originality of private and public autonomy. The suggested proceduralist paradigm of law would enable us to overcome the shortcomings of the other two legal paradigms:

> After the formal guarantee of private autonomy has proven insufficient, and after social intervention through law also threatens the very private autonomy it means to restore, the only solution consists in thematizing the connection between forms of communication that *simultaneously* guarantee private and public autonomy *in the very conditions from which they emerge*. (Habermas 1992 [1996]: 409)

The possibilities of bringing out this interrelation between private and public autonomy obviously depend on the political conjuncture. At the time of the publication of *Between Facts and Norms*, Habermas (1992 [1996]: 439) expressed his hopes in the following way:

> In the proceduralist paradigm, the vacancies left by the private-market participant and the client of welfare bureaucracies are filled by enfranchised citizens who participate in political discourses in order to address violated interests and, by articulating new needs, to collaborate in shaping standards for treating like cases alike and different cases differently.

Nothing seems more remote from this hope than the contemporary situation. The impact of neoliberal restructuring, certainly underway already in the early 1990s, has since then eroded several features of the democratic welfare state or significantly changed them. Privatisation of public services, inequalities in the provision of social rights, precarious labour conditions, concentration of wealth, and increasing social and economic inequalities are examples (see Brown 2015; Crouch 2004; Scheuerman 2013; Streeck 2012). Wolfgang Streeck (2012) stresses how the neoliberal structuring involves shifts from citizen to consumer, from voice to exit, and argues that one important background for these changes is the transformation from Fordist to post-Fordist consumption from the 1970s onwards. The diversified and individualised set of products on offer, combined with a growth in various types of services that enable wide individual choice, has had consequences for the public provision of goods. As Streeck (2012: 40) formulates it:

> [T]he restructuring of consumption aimed at restoring the dynamics of capitalist accumulation after the crisis of the 1970s made possible – indeed, invited and cultivated – attitudes and expectations on the part of customers-cum-citizens that inexorably began to radiate into what remained of the public sphere.

The transformations we have witnessed over the past few decades do not facilitate persons taking up the orientation required for acting as authors of law. Together with increasing insecurity and vulnerability, nowadays often discussed in terms of precarity, the risk of undermining the shared responsibilities central for democracy is obvious (see Näsström and Kalm 2014).

We may, of course, see the neoliberal transformation of the welfare state only in terms of the political conjuncture, but there is a pattern emerging. Both the liberal and the welfare state paradigms of law involved a focus on private autonomy. The same is the case with the neoliberal transformation of the welfare state. The pattern emerging is then that common to modern legal paradigms is the centrality of private autonomy. Habermas suggests that this is because the relation between private and public autonomy has not been properly clarified. However, there is another possible interpretation: the centrality of private autonomy found in modern paradigms of law is because modern law builds on rights tailored to private autonomy. Thus, we may say that it is perhaps less the troubles of showing the internal link between private and public autonomy that is the problem to address and instead the fact that modern law involves the emphasis on private autonomy. This is after all the common denominator of the liberal and the welfare state legal paradigms.

Again: Private and Public Autonomy

Habermas does not take seriously the interpretation that the reason we find the stressing of private autonomy in both the liberal and the welfare state paradigms of law is because modern law itself privileges this autonomy. He argues that this shows how both paradigms lose sight of public autonomy. While certainly diagnosing a central problem in both legal paradigms, it is far from self-evident that modern law is an adequate medium for clarifying the mutual relation between private and public autonomy.

Habermas is aware of this problem. When Habermas (1992 [1996]: 32) says citizens are '*not* allowed to take part' in lawmaking processes 'simply in the role of actors oriented to success', he recognises the risks involved if private autonomy becomes the prevalent attitude in politics. In the case it becomes so, politics is only a way of asserting one's own will and interests. This concern also lies behind his argument that 'individual liberties' should be 'supplemented by rights of *a different type*, rights of citizenship that are geared no longer to rational choice but to autonomy in the Kantian sense' (Habermas 1992 [1996]: 33). The problem, however, is that there are no such rights of a different type. Political rights enabling political participation are like all other rights. Even political rights are tailored to individual choice, the choice of participating or not (Luhmann 1981; Menke 2015). Thus, the reconstruction of private and public autonomy requires a kind of rights that do not exist as *rights*.

This is the crux of the matter. It is not surprising then that Habermas has to gesture to a citizenry accustomed to political freedom to help him support the idea that citizens should be oriented towards the common good in how they use their political rights. This orientation is both necessary and yet not possible to secure through rights. Thus, Habermas needs an orientation in how rights are used, which he cannot account for by explicating the system of rights that supposedly provide the conditions for the possibility of democratic lawmaking (compare Bernstein 1998; Dews 2002). There is a chasm between the orientation required and the conditions explicating its possibility. Habermas (2003 [2005]: 4) is certainly right that we should not impose legal obligations 'to be in solidarity'. He says that this would be a 'contradiction' and in this he is correct, but perhaps in ways he did not really intend with this expression. What turns out to be a contradiction is less a legal obligation to be in solidarity than the idea of closing the 'gap' in solidarity that rights tailored towards choice opens up through rights.[7] It is when noting this gap that Habermas argues for the need to have rights of a different type. As Peter Dews (2002: 177) argues, Habermas 'downplays the possibilities for conflict between law and solidarity'.

Habermas' focus on the legal medium in the light of absence of alternatives and the claims he makes about the 'marvels of law', to borrow a phrase from Rousseau, does not really add up. Besides the recognition of the centrality of private autonomy, consider how Habermas portrays the legal paradigms (compare Arato 1998). Habermas presents the procedural paradigm in terms of its potentials, how it would bring out the political autonomy of citizens. The presentation is oriented towards future possibilities. The presentation of the previous two paradigms follows another logic. Habermas presents them in terms of their institutionalisation. What then disappears are the political moments of these paradigms. This way of presenting, for instance, the welfare state paradigms means that it is the institutionalisation of labour movement demands that becomes central, not the political action of these movements. The result is an approach that simultaneously overemphasises the possibilities of resolving tensions between private and public autonomy through the procedural paradigm and underestimates the political action involved in bringing about the liberal and the welfare state paradigm. The institutionalisation of the liberal paradigm involved conflicts regarding public and private autonomy, for instance, discussed by Arendt (1963: Chap. 3) in terms of private and public happiness in the context of the American Revolution and its aftermath. The struggle for societal change in labour movements during the nineteenth and early twentieth centuries did not focus on private autonomy. On the contrary, the centrality of private autonomy in the welfare state is a consequence of how demands became institutionalised, not characteristic of these demands as such.

Thus, the problem is less that the liberal and the welfare state legal paradigms failed to bring out the co-originality of private and public autonomy than this being a problem in any modern legal paradigm. This interpretation is closer to Marx' (1843) discussion about the difference between revolutionary politics, aiming towards liberation, and the constitutional regulation of post-revolutionary politics. There is a chasm between liberation central to revolutionary politics and the legal form of freedom in the post-revolutionary constitutions. With this interpretation, there is a tension between the legal formulation of the conditions for legitimate lawmaking on the one hand and emancipation on the other hand. Habermas is right to insist on this connection but does not address the limitations of the language of law in realising it.

Conclusions

The reconstruction of the system of rights, which forms the kernel of the undertaking in *Between Facts and Norms*, addresses how citizens may program system media. This is certainly important because questions about how to regulate money and administrative power are pressing concerns for our own times. In explicating how this is possible through the system of rights, Habermas argues that law is a language for the realisation of autonomy. This understanding is problematic, though. The problems stem in my view from the fact that Habermas no longer attends to the dialectic of law. This makes his argument that law is language for autonomy less convincing. The problems of the colonisation analysis make it understandable why Habermas abandons it, but by not addressing the dialectic of law in other ways, he also forfeits conceptual tools for assessing the limitations of law being language of autonomy.

That such limitations exist is in ways suggested by Habermas, even though he does not draw out the consequences of his analysis. He argues that private autonomy is privileged in both the liberal and the welfare state paradigms. This entails losing sight of public autonomy. Habermas' ambition is to show the co-originality of private and public autonomy, but the stress of private autonomy found in both paradigms may suggest another conclusion, namely that this reflects characteristics of modern law. More specifically, the reason for the emphasis of private autonomy in modern legal paradigms is because the modern understanding of rights is conceptually tailored to individual choice. Habermas is certainly aware of the links between private autonomy and modern law and senses the problems of understanding political autonomy on this basis. Political autonomy requires another orientation than using rights for pursuing private interests. However, political rights central to this other orientation is not of a different type. They have the same form as other rights.

Notes

1. For a discussion, see Baxter (2011): 74f and Rehg and Bohman (2002).
2. Habermas (1992 [1996]: 92) argues that Kant saw that 'rights cannot for their part be grounded by recourse to a model taken from private law'. The social contract differs from contracts regulating exchange in what it found, a 'kind of sociation ruled by the principle of law', Habermas (1992 [1996]: 93) claims.
3. This is understandable given the problematic connotations of people, in particular, the German notion of 'Volk'. However, Habermas misrepresents the complex history of the notion of the people (see Agamben 1996). He relies on the distinction between ethno-cultural and republican interpretations, which underlie his defence of the republican conception in the discussion of 'constitutional patriotism' (see Habermas 1996). What disappears from view are then, for instance, the connection between people and poor as well as people as those not having power. The latter sense, Maus (1996: 874ff) points out, was central to the debates on popular sovereignty, in which people referred to those who had no position in the state apparatus, that is, those who were the non-functionaries (see also Maus 2011). For questions about the legitimacy of the people, see Näsström (2007).
4. Public spheres, Habermas (1992: Sect. 8.3) argues, are networks for communicating information; through them grievances, claims, suggestions and so on are articulated and to some extent synthesised into public opinions (see also Habermas 1962). Civil society plays a role in amplifying what emerges in public spheres (Habermas 1992: 435ff).
5. Habermas also relates his discussion to Nancy Fraser's (1990) account of weak and strong publics. This distinction largely concerns whether public spheres tie in with decision-making bodies or not. Weak publics do not, whereas strong publics do. This difference also means that the two types of public spheres have different functions and rationales. William Scheuerman (1999: 163ff) points to the problems of combining Fraser's and Peters' accounts. Fraser's account intends to work out a radical democratic conception of the role of publics, whereas Peter's views are closer to the realist democratic tradition.
6. It is, of course, far from certain that crises function in this way since they may also make large parts of the citizenry more passive. Crises may be pretext for undertaking decisive changes that curtail rights and transforms the state. Examples over the past few decades include security crises, in particular, post-September 11, 2001, and economic crises, which have played an important role for the neoliberal restructuring of welfare states over the past few decades.

7. Habermas (1992 [1996]: 32) formulates it in the following way: 'This gap in solidarity, which opens up insofar as legal subjects exclusively pursue their own private interests, cannot be closed again by rights tailored for this kind of success-oriented action, or at least not by such rights alone'.

References

Agamben, Giorgio. 1996 [2000]. *Means Without End. Notes on Politics*, trans. Vincenzo Binetti and Cesare Casarino. Minneapolis: University of Minnesota Press.

Arendt, Hannah. 1958. *The Human Condition*. Chicago: University of Chicago Press.

Arendt, Hannah. 1963 [1990]. *On Revolution*. London: Penguin.

Arendt, Hannah. 1969. *On Violence*. New York: Harcourt Brace.

Arato, Andrew. 1998. Procedural Law and Civil Society. In *Habermas on Law and Democracy: Critical Exchanges*, ed. Michel Rosenfeld and Andrew Arato, 26–36. Berkeley: University of California Press.

Bachrach, Peter, and Aryeh Botwinick. 1992. *Power and Empowerment. A Radical Theory of Participatory Democracy*. Philadelphia: Temple University Press.

Baxter, Hugh. 2011. *Habermas: The Discourse Theory of Law and Democracy*. Stanford: Stanford University Press.

Benjamin, Walter. 1921 [1965]. Zur Kritik der Gewalt. In *Zur Kritik der Gewalt und andere Aufsätze*, ed. Herbert Marcuse, 29–65. Frankfurt: Suhrkamp.

Bernstein, Richard. 1998. The Retrieval of the Democratic Ethos. In *Habermas on Law and Democracy: Critical Exchanges*, ed. Michel Rosenfeld and Andrew Arato, 287–305. Berkeley: University of California Press.

Bohman, James. 2000. *Public Deliberation: Pluralism, Complexity, and Democracy*. Cambridge, MA: MIT Press.

Brown, Wendy. 2015. *Undoing the Demos. Neoliberalism's Stealth Revolution*. New York: Zone Books.

Cordero, Rodrigo. 2014. Crisis and Critique in Jürgen Habermas's Social Theory. *European Journal of Social Theory* 17 (4): 497–515.

Crouch, Colin. 2004. *Post-Democracy*. Cambridge: Polity.

Dahl, Robert. 1989. *Democracy and its Critics*. New Haven: Yale University Press.

Dahl, Robert. 2007. *On Political Equality*. New Haven: Yale University Press.

Deflem, Mathieu. 1994. Introduction: Law in Habermas's Theory of Communicative Action. *Philosophy & Social Criticism* 20 (4): 1–20.

Deflem, Mathieu. 2008. *Sociology of Law. Visions of a Scholarly Tradition*. Cambridge: Cambridge University Press.

Demirovic, Alex. 1997. Zivilgesellschaft, Öffentlichkeit, Demokratie. Demokratie und Herrschaft. Aspekter kritischer Gesellschaftstheorie. *Demirovic*, 148–164. Münster: Westfälisches Dampfboot.

Dews, Peter. 2002. Law, Solidarity, and the Tasks of Philosophy. In *Discourse and Democracy. Essays on Habermas's Between Facts and Norms*, ed. René von Schomberg and Kenneth Baynes, 165–184. Albany: State University of New York Press.

Fraser, Nancy. 1990. Rethinking the Public Sphere: A Contribution to the Critique of Actually Existing Democracy. *Social Text* 25 (26): 56–80.

Fung, Archon, and Erik Olin Wright (eds.). 2003. *Deepening Democracy. Institutional Innovations in Empowered Participatory Governance*. London: Verso.

Giddens, Anthony. 1985. *The Nation-State and Violence. A Contemporary Critique of Historical Materialism*, vol. 2. Cambridge: Polity.

Giugni, Marco, Doug McAdam, and Charles Tilly (eds.). 1999. *How Social Movements Matter*. Minneapolis: University of Minnesota Press.

Günther, Klaus. 1994. Diskurstheorie des Rechts oder Naturrecht in diskurstheoretischen Gewande. *Kritische Justiz* 27 (4): 470–487.

Günther, Klaus. 1998. Communicative Freedom, Communicative Power, and Jurisgenesis. In *Habermas on Law and Democracy: Critical Exchanges*, ed. Michel Rosenfeld and Andrew Arato, 234–254. Berkeley: University of California Press.

Habermas, Jürgen. 1962 [1990]. *Strukturwandel der Öffentlichkeit*. Frankfurt: Suhrkamp.

Habermas, Jürgen. 1973. *Legitimationsprobleme im Spätkapitalismus*. Frankfurt: Suhrkamp.

Habermas, Jürgen. 1983. Diskursethik – Notizen zu einem Begründungsprogramm. In *Moralbewusstsein und kommunikatives Handeln*, ed. Jürgen Habermas, 53–125. Frankfurt: Suhrkamp.

Habermas, Jürgen. 1985. *Der philosophische Diskurs der Moderne*. Frankfurt: Suhrkamp.

Habermas, Jürgen. 1991. *Erläuterungen zur Diskursethik*. Frankfurt: Suhrkamp.

Habermas, Jürgen. 1992 [1996]. *Faktizität und Geltung. Beiträge zur Diskurstheorie des Rechts und des demokratischen Rechtsstaats*. Frankfurt: Suhrkamp. Translated by William Rehg as *Between Facts and Norms. Contributions to a Discourse Theory of Law and Democracy*. Cambridge: Polity Press.

Habermas, Jürgen. 1996. Inklusion – Einbeziehen order Einschliessen? Zum Verhältnis von Nation, Rechtsstaat und Demokratie. In *Die Einbeziehung des Anderen. Studien zur politischen Theorie*, ed. Habermas, 154–184. Frankfurt: Suhrkamp.

Habermas, Jürgen. 2003 [2005]. Kulturelle Gleichbehandlung – und die Grenzen des Postmodernen Liberalismus. In *Zwischen Naturalismus und Religion. Philosophische Aufsätze*, ed. Jürgen Habermas, 279–323. Frankfurt: Suhrkamp. Translated as 'Equal Treatment of Cultures and the Limits of Postmodern Liberalism'. *The Journal of Political Philosophy* 13 (1): 1–28.

Habermas, Jürgen. 2011. *Zur Verfassung Europas. Ein Essay*. Berlin: Suhrkamp.

Honneth, Axel. 2011 [2014]. *Das Recht der Freiheit. Grundriss einer demokratischen Sittlichkeit*. Berlin: Suhrkamp. Translated by Joseph Ganahl as *Freedom's Right. The Social Foundations of Democratic Life*. Cambridge: Polity.

Kupka, Thomas. 1994. Jürgen Habermas diskurstheoretische Reformuliering des klassichen Vernunftrechts. *Kritische Justiz* 27 (4): 461–469.

Larmore, Charles. 1993. Die Wurzeln radikaler Demokratie. *Deutsche Zeitschift für Philosphie* 41 (2): 321–328.

Loughlin, Martin. 2010. *Foundations of Public Law*. Oxford: Oxford University Press.

Luhmann, Niklas. 1981. Subjektive Rechte: Zum Umbau des Rechtsbewusstseins für die modern Gesellschaft. In *Gesellschaftsstruktur und Semantik. Studien zur Wissenssoziologie der modernen Gesellschaft. Band 2*, ed. Niklas Luhmann, 45–104. Frankfurt: Suhrkamp.

Manin, Bernhard. 1997. *The Principles of Representative Government*. Cambridge: Cambridge University Press.

Maus, Ingeborg. 1996. Liberties and Popular Sovereignty: On Jürgen Habermas's Reconstruction of the System of Rights. *Cardozo Law Review* 17 (4–5): 825–882.

Maus, Ingeborg. 2011. *Über Volkssouveränität*. Berlin: Suhrkamp.

Marx, Karl. 1843 [1977]. Zur Judenfrage. In *Marx-Engels Werke*, vol. 1, 347–377. Berlin: Dietz Verlag. Translation by Gregor Benton as On the Jewish Question. In Karl Marx, *Early Writings*, 211–242. London: Penguin 1992.

Menke, Christoph. 2010. Law and Violence. *Law and Literature* 22 (1): 1–17.

Menke, Christoph. 2015. *Kritik der Rechte*. Berlin: Suhrkamp.

Näsström, Sofia. 2007. The Legitimacy of the People. *Political Theory* 35 (5): 624–658.

Näsström, Sofia, and Sara Kalm. 2014. A democratic critique of precarity. *Global Discourse: An Interdisciplinary Journal of Current Affairs and Applied Contemporary Thought* 5 (4): 556–573.

Offe, Claus. 1989. Fessel und Bremse. In *Zwischenbetrachtungen im Prozess the Aufklärung*, ed. Axel Honneth et al., 739–774. Frankfurt: Suhrkamp.

Olson, Kevin. 1998. 'Democratic Inequalities: The Problem of Equal Citizenship in Habermas' Democratic Theory. *Constellations* 5 (2): 215–233.

Peters, Bernhard. 1993. *Die Integration moderner Gesellschaften*. Frankfurt: Suhrkamp.

Preuss, Ulrich. 1998. Communicative Power and the Concept of Law. In *Habermas on Law and Democracy: Critical Exchanges*, ed. Michel Rosenfeld and Andrew Arato, 323–335. Berkeley: University of California Press.

Rawls, Jon. 1993. *Political Liberalism*. New York: Columbia University Press.

Rehg, William, and James Bohman. 2002. Discourse and Democracy: The Formal and the Informal Bases of Legitimacy in *Between Facts and Norms*. In *Discourse and Democracy. Essays on Habermas's Between Facts and Norms*, ed. René von Schomberg and Kenneth Baynes, 31–60. Albany: State University of New York Press.

Scheuerman, William. 1999. Between Radicalism and Resignation: Democratic Theory in Habermas's Between Facts and Norms. In *Habermas: A Critical Reader*, ed. Peter Dews, 153–177. Oxford: Blackwell.

Scheuerman, William. 2013. Capitalism, Law, and Social Criticism. *Constellations* 20 (4): 571–686.

Staats, Joseph. 2004. Habermas and Democratic Theory: The Threat to Democracy of Unchecked Corporate Power. *Political Research Quarterly* 57 (4): 585–594.

Streeck, Wolfgang. 2012. Citizens as Customers. Considerations on the New Politics of Consumption. *New Left Review* 76: 27–47.

Tarrow, Sidney. 1998. *Power in Movement: Social Movements and Contentious Politics*. Cambridge: Cambridge University Press.

Tilly, Charles (ed.). 1975. *The Formation of National States in Western Europe*. Princeton: Princeton University Press.

Tilly, Charles. 1992. *Coercion, Capital, and European States, AD 990–1992*. Oxford: Blackwell.

Tilly, Charles. 2013. *Social Movements 1768–2004*. Boulder: Paradigm Publishers.

Touri, Kaarlo. 1989. Discourse Ethics and the Legitimacy of Law. *Ratio Juris* 2 (2): 125–143.

CHAPTER 5

Conclusions

Abstract This chapter briefly presents the conclusion of the study, discussing the relevance of considering the dialectic of law in the context of Habermas' theorising of law, rights and democracy and the extent to which Habermas makes good on his claims to have shown the co-originality of private and public autonomy. The latter is important in itself but primarily of interest at the background of the shift from the analysis of law in *The Theory of Communicative Action* to that in *Between Facts and Norms*. In the latter work, Habermas argues that the dilemma of welfare state law is understandable as the dialectic of legal and factual equality. To interpret the dilemma in this way presupposes showing the co-originality of private and public autonomy.

Keywords Habermas · Democracy · Autonomy · Law · Rights

In this study, I have discussed Habermas' analyses of law in modern societies with a specific focus on his claims that by reconstructing the relation between private and public autonomy; we understand the meaning of constitutional democracy and can clarify how this project serves emancipatory purposes. Habermas argues that his reconstruction allows for legal consociates to work out understandings of emancipated forms of life. This claim builds on the assumption that law is the language for the realisation of autonomy. I have suggested that when discussing this claim, we need to take into account the modern critique of law. This

M. Spång, *Emancipation, Democracy and the Modern Critique of Law*, International Political Theory, DOI 10.1007/978-3-319-62890-5_5

tradition has since Marx directed attention to the limitations of assuming that law is the language of autonomy and rights are the vocabulary of emancipation. Among the several ways this has been discussed, the most interesting and convincing is in my view the discussion about the dialectic of law.

The statement that law is condition for both emancipation and domination is usually discussed in relation to private law liberalism and welfare state law, the two main paradigms of modern law. Marx focused on private law, addressing the relation between legal equality and capitalist exploitation. This focus on private law is understandable in the background of its importance until the late nineteenth and early twentieth centuries, but it also made it difficult for scholars in the Marxian tradition to address welfare state law. Yet, some theorists in the late twentieth century attempted to analyse welfare state law through the lens of the dialectic of law. Habermas is one of them. In *The Theory of Communicative Action*, he addresses how freedom and normalisation relate to each other, making welfare state law dilemmatic. Habermas claims that the dilemma of welfare state law is intrinsic to this phase of juridification. In *Between Facts and Norms*, Habermas thinks that this characterisation was too rash. While normalisation tied to welfare state law continues to be one of Habermas' concerns, he no longer theorises it in terms of the dialectic of law. Instead, he suggests understanding it as a matter of the dialectic of legal and factual equality, the relationship between de jure and de facto equality key to the materialisation of law.

The reason welfare state law is not dilemmatic, as such, Habermas argues, is because the criteria for assessing when welfare state law turns from promoting to restricting freedom are given by the reconstruction of private and public autonomy. This means that citizens' political participation becomes important. The extent to which citizens are involved in law- and policymaking is one criterion for assessing welfare state measures. Another criterion is given by private autonomy. Welfare state measures are restricting when severely affecting persons' abilities to develop life plans of their own. The conclusion is that while the materialisation of law leads to the problems of normalisation, law is at the same time medium for resolving these problems. In contrast, the colonisation analysis implies that there are limitations to the legal medium, and the dilemmatic character of welfare state law implies that law is an ambivalent medium. In *Between Facts and Norms*, Habermas draws another conclusion. Normalisation does not affect the conclusion that law is the language for the realisation of autonomy because the possibilities of overcoming restrictions to freedom are themselves contained in the legal medium.

There are several merits to Habermas' approach in *Between Facts and Norms*, especially of course bringing out the importance of citizens being authors of the law. Clarifying the meaning and implication of self-legislation by citizens in functionally differentiated societies is much needed. However, in clarifying the conditions for the possibility of constitutional democracy, it is also relevant to consider the limitations of this project. One type of limitation concerns whether self-legislation by citizens is 'realistic' given what we know about political processes, the influence of corporations and interest organisations on legislation, etc. Another type of criticism, partly also focused on the realism of this idea, follows from considerations of modern society being functionally differentiated. A prominent example is the social theory of Luhmann, which implies that self-legislation by citizens builds on ideas that are no longer relevant. Yet another kind of limitation is that which I have addressed in this study, law being condition for both emancipation and domination.

Taking this into account means to direct critical attention to the claim Habermas advances in *Between Facts and Norms*, namely that the law is the language of autonomy. Attending to the ways in which law also enables the institutionalisation of domination, how welfare state law makes possible both freedom and normalisation, implies that we cannot assume that law is this kind of language. At least, this assumption needs qualification. It does not mean discarding this language, to say that it only serves for the purposes of domination. It is true that sometimes this is the conclusion drawn by scholars in the tradition of the modern critique of law. Legal equality, for instance, was discarded as semblance by many Marxists, pointing to its ideological dimensions. Most contemporary theorists that belong to the modern critique of law, for instance, Brown, Buckel and Menke, however, do not engage in this reductionist analysis. Instead, they want to point out the paradoxes and ambivalences of the legal medium in the light of its importance to much of contemporary political theorising as well as public debates.

I have tried to show how Habermas takes the dialectic of law seriously in *The Theory of Communicative Action*. There are certainly problems regarding how Habermas develops this analysis, the colonisation of the lifeworld. These problems make it understandable why he abandons it. However, Habermas does not replace it with other conceptual tools for understanding the dialectic of law. This means that there is a need for formulating the dialectic of law in other ways. I have suggested that Menke's analysis of the modern form of rights and the modern legal form is useful in this regard because it makes it possible to address normalisation in welfare state law without relying on the lifeworld system distinction. Menke's analysis is also of relevance because he directs attention to the role of private autonomy for the development of modern law and the modern conception of rights.

The role of private autonomy in modern law is relevant when considering the reconstruction of private and public autonomy. As stated, Habermas argues that the reason the characterisation of welfare state law as intrinsically dilemmatic was too rash is that the criteria for assessing the turn from autonomy to its opposite are given by the reconstruction. However, to the extent rights, which play a key role in Habermas' reconstruction, which are closely linked to private autonomy, we may ask, is this not affecting the possibilities of showing private and public autonomy being co-original? Habermas stresses the need for understanding political autonomy in other ways than the pursuit of private interests, the strategic calculation of law as outer restrictions, and so on. He argues that there is a need for a different type of rights. This different type of rights would clarify political partaking. The problem is that there is no such different kind of rights. Political rights are not of a different type; they are conceptually the same as other modern rights. This creates problems for reconstructing the mutual supporting relation between private and public autonomy through a system of rights.

This problem also explains why Habermas vacillates between arguing for the need for a different kind of rights to make sense of political participation and him stressing the differences in how rights are used. Certainly, political rights can be used in ways that are not about pursuing private interests but instead orientated towards the common good and the general interest. Habermas here thinks that his reconstruction builds on a citizenry accustomed to political freedom, but there is a chasm between this and the way he explains the conditions for the possibility of political participation. The orientation towards the common good is not explicated through the outlining of the conditions for its possibility. The latter, the suggested system of rights, enables both civic privatism and political participation.

This problem of the reconstruction of private and public autonomy suggests a different conclusion to the one Habermas draws. When

Habermas observes that both the liberal and the welfare state legal paradigms involve an emphasis on private autonomy, it is true that this shows how they lose sight of public autonomy. However, to conclude from this that we can show the co-originality of private and public autonomy through the legal medium is far from self-evident. We may draw the opposite conclusion, namely that this shows the problems of bringing out the meaning of political autonomy through the legal medium. In my view, this is relevant to address. In the case we want to outline the conditions for the possibility of political participation, we need to understand the limitations of the medium, modern law, in doing so. Otherwise, we are not enlightening ourselves about the possibilities of political autonomy.

Index

M. Spång, *Emancipation, Democracy and the Modern Critique of Law*, International Political Theory, DOI 10.1007/978-3-319-62890-5